The Father Loves

Look Inside God's Heart
2nd Edition

By Linda Patarello

Unless otherwise indicated, all Scripture quotations are taken from the *KJV Reference Bible.* Copyright © 2000 by Zondervan. Used by permission.

Scripture quotations marked AMP are taken from the *Amplified® Bible.* Copyright © 1954, 1958, 1962, 1964, 1965, 1987 by The Lockman Foundation. Used by permission. (www.Lockman.org).

Scripture quotations marked NIV are taken from The Holy Bible: New International Version® NIV®. Copyright © 1973, 1978, 1984, by International Bible Society. Used by permission of Zondervan Publishing House. All rights reserved.

Scripture quotations marked NLT are taken from *The Holy Bible, New Living Translation®.* Copyright © 1996, 2004, 2007. Used by permission of Tyndale House Publishers, Inc.

Scripture quotations marked MSG are taken from *The Message.* Copyright © 1993, 1994, 1995, 1996, 2000, 2001, 2002. Used by permission of NavPress Publishing Group.

The Father Loves, 2nd Edition
ISBN: 978-0-9896919-0-1

Editor: DeAnne Ussrey

Published by Orion Productions, LLC.
P.O. Box 51194
Colorado Springs, CO 80949
Orionproductions.tv

Printed in the United States of America. This book or parts thereof may not be reproduced in any form, stored in a retrieval system, or transmitted in any form by any means—electronic, mechanical, photocopy, recording, or otherwise—without prior written permission from the Publisher.

CONTENTS

Foreword

Prologue

A Father Who Loves 19

A Father Of Mercy And Comfort 35

God Has Emotions 47

Our Father Sees And Hears Us 65

The Father Knows All About You 79

Relationship? But I Can't See Him 89

Our Aim Is To Know God 111

The Father Wants You To Trust Him 123

Let God Speak 139

God Sings Over You 151

God Gave His Best Gift 167

What Pleases Your Father? 179

Living In The Faith Realm Of The Father 195

Receive Jesus As Your Savior 209

Foreword

In this powerful treatise, Linda dispels the misunderstandings and traditional religious thinking that characterizes most people's understanding of God's love. As I read this book, I found myself feeling more secure in my understanding that God really does love me.

Linda handles the difficult issue of emotions with great care and gives us a greater understanding of the fact that God Himself possesses emotions, and how He intends for us to live with ours. With the support of Scripture, she deftly gives examples of how God intended our emotions to bless and enhance the experience of His love in our lives.

As Linda weaves together faith and love, a superior picture emerges of who God wants me to be in this life. I came away with a greater understanding of what really pleases God and a deeper revelation of the fact that God is Love. He doesn't have love nor does He manufacture love. It is the core of His nature, and that love is trained on you and me.

I believe that when a Christian receives the greater revelation that God truly loves them, then most questions and difficulties experienced in living the Christian life begin to disappear. I highly recommend this book to anyone who wants a greater revelation of God's love and who wants to be free to experience the joy of living wrapped in the Father's love.

Paul Milligan, Director
Charis Bible College School of Business
Andrew Wommack Ministries Board of Directors

Special Testimony From The Father Loves

Dear Linda,

My name is Michael. I want to thank you for writing your book, The Father Loves. It helped me understand what God wanted from me, and what I wanted from Him. It also taught me alot about my relationship with the Father. I now speak with Him and find myself thinking of Him before I speak, and doing things I never did before. I now know He's always listening, watching, and cares about me and what happens to me. Thanks to a friend of mine at the prison who gave me this book, I understand your book, and I know how to respond to it. I really mean it when I say that I enjoyed your book because it has already started to change my life. Thank you again for helping me, and probably tons of other people in the future (from a correctional facility in California).

Sincerely,

Michael

Endorsements

In Linda's book on The Father Loves, she presents that God is interested in our everyday lives. His love for us goes far beyond the church doors. Linda's life is a great representation of the Father's love on display for the world to see.

Lawson Perdue, Pastor
Charis Christian Center

Only One can satisfy, only One can love you back to wholeness. We need to know the love of The Father. There are many who do not know the love of a father, much less the love of God. There are those who have not had a true relationship with their father, nor with their Heavenly Father. And, there are those who just need to be reminded about how much God loves them. Whoever you are, you will be touched by the Almighty Father's love in this wonderfully written book, The Father Loves.

Kathryn Hanson
CBC Co-Director, San Jose, CA

Acknowledgements

I'd like to thank, first of all, my wonderful family back home who willingly let me leave and move to Colorado to attend Bible school. Without their great understanding, this book never would have been written. I love you all. I know it wasn't easy. Thank you Dad, Mom, Dan, Ernie, Linda, Aaron, Dani, Heather, Amy and Ernie.

Thanks to my friends Dan and Sheri, for helping me move to Colorado, and lugging all my furniture in the U-Haul up those crazy hills. Your support I will never forget.

Thanks to my kids for being you. Aaron, Lauren and my son-in-law Justin; you are treasures to me. I love you. Thanks to Ron for your support while I've been in Bible College; we are being restored and mended with God's help.

Thanks to Pastor Don and Vicky for letting me leave my post as worship leader to come here.

Thanks to my friends Linda, Dilfuza and Joyce for encouraging me to write this book. You inspired me, as you urged me on.

Thanks to one of my teachers at Charis Bible College, Delron Shirley, for reading over some of the chapters to give me your wise input.

Thanks to my roomie Sylvia for understanding when I wouldn't go hiking because I was locked away typing.

Thanks to my teachers Greg Mohr, Paul Milligan and Daniel Amstutz for your leadership and wise counsel and support, I respect you greatly. From you I have learned about servanthood and humility.

Thank you, Andrew Wommack, for your obedience to start this school, Charis Bible College; God has used you to change my life indeed, and I will never be the same!

Thank you, my sweet Heavenly Father, for calling me to write about your precious love. Your heart is for all to know how deeply you love us! Your quest will be my quest. It is for you that I run! To my loving Savior, Jesus, who died so I could have abundant life; that I would let you live strong through me and always let you be my delight. To the Holy Spirit, my Comforter, my Guide and Friend, let your power rest on this book and bring it into those hands that need it.

Prologue

After I was saved, the subject of the love of God and knowing the Father intrigued me; and with such a hunger, I began to search. Whenever I heard of someone teaching on these subjects, my ears would perk up; they had my full attention. During my search, however, I noticed that there was not much teaching available on the Father's love. We talk a lot about our wonderful Savior, Jesus; how we can do works in His name, and that He died for us on the cross, which is God's greatest act of love to us.

We long to be closer to our Savior and to walk in His ways. Still, not much has been written about the love of our Heavenly Father—more people need to know about Him. Many believe, and have been taught, that He is a mean, cross God, Who is just waiting to strike us with His masterful lightning bolt. WRONG. He is so the opposite of what many have portrayed Him to be.

One day, as a Charis Bible College student, I was being taught about the Heavenly Father, and it felt so amazingly refreshing to me, like a cool glass of water on a hot summer afternoon.

That night, as I meditated on the teaching, I wanted more. I craved to know more about our Father. In all honesty, I realized that I didn't know how to relate to Him as a Father. Quite frankly, I don't think that most Christians do.

In the day in which we live, the standard role of the earthly father is quite lacking. Broken homes and prisons are full of people who have never known their fathers. If you talk to many inmates (male or female) their fathers were gone, nonexistent, unknown, or abusive. Concerning female inmates, the loss of their fathers created a profuse amount of promiscuity, resulting from their longing to look for love in *all* of the wrong places. The current outlook of good fathers is dismal. We need fathers to stand up and take their place. Thank you, God, for the many fathers who *have* stood up and taken their place in the home and for ministries such as Promise Keepers, who strengthen and encourage fathers in rearing their children.

However, the problem I'm trying to explain is because of the growing rate of missing fathers on this earth, how can we relate to God as a father? It is impossible to enjoy what we don't know or cannot understand. Out of my own need to know and understand God as my father, I finally called out to Him and asked, "Help me to know You as 'Father.' What are You like? How are your ways similar to that of a true father's? How should I relate to you? If you're not the mean ogre that people portray you to be, then who are you?"

Thus began my quest. I know that the best way to know Jesus is by the Word of God. So, the best way to know the Father is by His Word. In my earnestness and lack of knowledge, I began a word study on the word "father." Then, I decided to search the Scriptures for His personality traits—His likes and dislikes; what is it that makes Him tick? Once I could figure out these details, then *just maybe* I could understand Him.

I made some charts with legal pads, and taped them together. I scribbled columns and headings with different character traits, listing Scriptures underneath each supporting trait. The more I studied and charted the Scriptures, the more there were—it was endless! I told God one day, "You are so big! How can I possibly capture You?"

I became enraptured with Him as a loving Father; a Living God full of mercy and goodness Who desires to be a big part of my life. My trust in Him grew and my relationship with Him flourished even more. I believe that getting to know God's love is an endless journey because there is so much to learn. He is infinite! How wonderful it is to think that we can continuously be seeking and growing in His love.

It is with great joy that I am able to share with you what I have learned about the Father's love. I prayed and asked the Holy Spirit to guide me, and to cause this book to flow. So, open your heart. I trust you will enjoy the ride…

Chapter 1

A FATHER WHO LOVES

He is so vast and complex, so deep and limitless. God is great and powerful and majestic. Where does one start? Let's look at how the Bible describes God: the Bible says that GOD is LOVE (1 John 4:8). Think about this a moment. It could have said that God is peace (which He is) but it did not say that. It clearly says that God is Love. God gave His Son for us because of His great love (John 3:16). However, He doesn't just love you and I; HE IS LOVE. So, we must set out to discover what this Love is.

Let's embark on a wonderful journey—a new adventure. Put aside the religion you've been taught in the past, and all of the memories, concepts, and perceptions you have ever imagined or been taught. Why, even put aside some of the "truths" you have believed from your parents about God, if they are contrary to His word. Take a fresh, new look now. Open your eyes to the light of the glorious gospel.

God's Personality

Would you like to know about God's personality? The Bible does explain His character. If God is Love, then you need to find where "Love" is explained. The place where it is most clearly explained is 1 Corinthians 13:4-8:

> *"Love endures long and is patient and kind; love never is envious nor boils over with jealousy, is not boastful or vainglorious, does not display itself haughtily.[4] It is not conceited (arrogant and inflated with pride); it is not rude (unmannerly) and does not act unbecomingly. Love (God's love in us) does not insist on its own rights or its own way, for it is not self-seeking; it is not touchy or fretful or resentful; it takes no account of the evil done to it [it pays no attention to a suffered wrong].[5] It does not rejoice at injustice and unrighteousness, but rejoices when right and truth prevail.[6] Love bears up under anything and everything that comes, is ever ready to believe the best of every person, its hopes are fadeless under all circumstances, and it endures*

everything [without weakening].⁷ Love never fails [never fades out or becomes obsolete or comes to an end]."⁸

Amplified

Now, if God is Love, then this verse describes exactly the way He loves you. Suppose we place the word, 'God' wherever the word, 'Love' is. Let's make this personal, just for you:

"GOD endures long and is patient and kind (with me); GOD never is envious nor boils over with jealousy, is not boastful or vainglorious, does not display Himself haughtily.⁴ HE is not conceited (arrogant and inflated with pride); HE is not rude (unmannerly) and does not act unbecomingly (with me). GOD...does not insist on HIS own rights or HIS own way, for HE is not self-seeking; HE is not touchy or fretful or resentful; HE takes no account of the evil (I've) done to HIM [...pays no attention to a suffered wrong] (from me).⁵ HE does not rejoice at injustice and unrighteousness, but rejoices when right and truth prevail (in my life).⁶ GOD bears up under anything and everything that comes, is ever ready to

> *believe the best (of me), HIS hopes are fadeless (for me) under all circumstances, and HE endures everything [without weakening].⁷ GOD never fails [never fades out or becomes obsolete or comes to an end]."⁸*

This is a far cry from how we have been taught to picture God; but, the Word does not lie. GOD IS LOVE. You need to say these Scriptures in 1 Corinthians until you believe them; until you are so convinced deep down in your heart that no one can ever persuade you otherwise.

According to this passage in First Corinthians, He has your best interests at heart; He is a giver and is not self-seeking; when you make a mistake, He pays no attention to it; He keeps on loving you; He doesn't make fun of you when you mess up; He sees the best in you. In fact, He is your biggest cheerleader. No matter what you do or what you go through or how many times you mess up, He only loves you. And His love never fails.

We've Been Adopted

We have also been adopted into His kingdom.

"Having predestinated us unto the adoption of children by Jesus Christ to himself, according to the good pleasure of his will."

Ephesians 1:5

If I were a child living in an orphanage, and someone wanted to adopt me, I would be overjoyed and overwhelmed. But most of all, I would want to know three things: that they would love me, want me, and never give me back. Basically, I would need to be assured of my security, and that my new parents would keep me. You can picture yourself in this state because that is what has really happened to us. That is if you have been able to accept Jesus as your Lord and Savior. We have been adopted into the wonderful kingdom of God. God, your Father, is excited about you, His own child. But, the door we must first walk through is Jesus.

Jesus said in John 14:6,

"I am the way, the truth, and the life: no man cometh unto the Father, but by me."

He said in John 3:16,

"For God so loved the world, that he gave his only begotten Son, that whosoever believeth in him should not perish, but have everlasting life."

Remember the verse in Ephesians that we just read? How He pre-destinated us unto the adoption of children according to the good pleasure of His will? He planned this long ago, even before the foundation of the world, and it gave Him great pleasure to adopt you. Most of the time when children are adopted, they are desperately wanted; the new parents are so excited that they cannot wait to get their new child. They have carefully decorated their room and have many plans and hopes and dreams for them. God has many plans, hopes and dreams for you, too, my friend. Believe it. Even before the foundation of the world, He chose you to be His very own.

Read it for yourself:

"Blessed be the God and Father of our Lord Jesus Christ, who hath blessed us with all spiritual blessings in heavenly places in Christ:[3] according as he hath chosen us in him before the foundation of the world, that we should be holy and without blame before him in love."[4]

Ephesians 1:3-4

It is worthy to comment about that last part of this verse, "that we should be holy and without blame before Him in love." There is no way that we could ever attain this holiness on our own. It is because of the finished work of Jesus Christ on the cross, that WE DO stand holy and without blame before Him in love. Amen! It *is* finished!

We were lost and born into sin so God had to find a way to get us back. He is holy and could not adopt us when we were in sin. Someone had to free us from our sins. Of course, there is no one on earth that could fit that bill!

> *"For God sent not his Son into the world to condemn the world; but that the world through him might be saved."*
>
> **John 3:17**

You may have heard these Scriptures many times before, but open your heart and see them again in a different light, knowing the Father's heart. This foundation (or understanding) must be laid before we go further. *If you need to stop reading in order to fully understand any of this, please take the time for yourself.*

> *"To the praise of the glory of his grace, wherein he hath made us accepted in the beloved.[6] In whom we have redemption through his blood, the forgiveness of sins, according to the riches of his grace."[7]*
>
> **Ephesians 1:6-7**

Just as a young couple needs to prepare for their child's arrival, so has God prepared for you. You are not only accepted, but you are deeply loved and anticipated for.

Don't ever think that He is too busy for you or that there are others that need more attention. Or maybe you think that there are others that should come before you. God gave His most valuable possession for you. That makes YOU a most valued treasure! Meditate on this truth, this kind of LOVE.

Many people were not brought up in a family with love because their parents were not loved. So, if someone was not loved nor taught how to love, how could they possibly love someone else?

Most of us live the way that we have been taught until someone teaches us the right way. This insight can help you to forgive you parents, other family or friends. In many ways, they didn't know any better. But know this: God knew you before you were born and His thoughts toward you have always been thoughts of love. Make no mistake about that. He sees your imperfections, but He still loves and forgives you.

Our Father thought of everything in detail, being careful not to miss a thing. Even when we were deep in sin, the Father gave His Son for you and me. That meant sending Jesus to become our sacrifice. Allowing Jesus to take thirty-nine lashes that belonged to us; that meant Jesus going to hell on our behalf. Remember that Jesus had to leave His special place of communion with God, His Father in order to die for us on the cross.

> *"But when the fulness of the time was come, God sent forth his Son, made of a woman, made under the law,[4] to redeem them that were under the law, that we might receive the adoption of sons.[5] And because ye are sons, God hath sent forth the Spirit of his Son into your hearts, crying, Abba, Father.[6] Wherefore thou art no more a servant, but a son; and if a son, then an heir of God through Christ."[7]*
>
> **Galatians 4:4-7**

Grasp this great truth, so that no one can ever convince you otherwise: GOD IS LOVE.

Drink of His Love

> *"For the Father himself loveth you, because ye have loved me, and have believed that I came out from God."*
>
> **John 16:27**

Put your name there, Dear One. Write it down on an index card and carry it with you. Say it, memorize it, and get it deep into your heart until it becomes real. This is bread; this is spiritual food. Nourish yourself, friend, for very likely you are as I was, having been starved so long of the love of the Father. It's going to take some time.

Be patient with yourself. You could read this book today. Tomorrow, you could forget the message because of being and feeling so lost, alone, and unloved.

The reason you have been love-starved is because you have been seeking for it from the wrong source! You must go to the source...God. If we continue looking to man to be our complete source of love, we will continue to starve. Man is incapable of God's unconditional love, even a man who is saved with their cup overflowing in the love of God. We need more than that; we need endless amounts of love to flow. Like Niagara Falls! God's love is limitless and He can only give you the love you have been looking for and so desperately need.

What Is Real Life?

"And this is life eternal, that they might know thee the only true God, and Jesus Christ, whom thou hast sent."

John 17:3

The Greek word for "know" is Ginosko, which means, "To come to know, to perceive, recognize or understand" (Strong's #1097).

Here is the same verse in the Amplified version:

"And this is eternal life: [it means] to know (to perceive, recognize, become acquainted with, and understand) You, the only true and real God, and [likewise] to know Him, Jesus [as the] Christ (the Anointed One, the Messiah), Whom You have sent."

John 17:3

The Word plainly says that eternal life is to know God; however, some of us have been brought up to understand that eternal life means that someday we are going to live forever with

God in heaven. But the Scripture says that real life is knowing Him. Can you imagine getting to know the One Who created you? This is the ultimate experience that life has to offer!

People have many ideas of what "real life" is. Some picture themselves basking in a lounge chair on the white smooth sands of the Bahamas, sipping a fancy cocktail with a little umbrella, saying, "Ahhhh, this is the life!"

Others may say, "Someday, when I have more money, a better job, and more respect I will have 'made it!'" Or, "When I win the lottery..."

NO, this is the life. KNOWING GOD is the real life. You don't have to wait until you get to heaven. God didn't send His Son just so that we could have eternal life in the sweet by and by! He wants us to enjoy the presence of the Holy Spirit right now, today! Nothing, absolutely nothing can compare to it!

Eternal Life is knowing and becoming acquainted with God. I am speaking of a real love relationship with your Creator. We all yearn to be loved and accepted. Without God, there is a hole inside of us that only His unconditional love can fill. He made you and I to be dependent creatures, but to be dependent upon Him. Not on money, drugs, the opposite sex, and other substitutes. Jesus Christ, the only true living God can only fill that void you feel.

When you have a revelation of God's love and begin nurturing your relationship with Him, this is what you will experience: more peace, true security, more smiles and a skip in your step; you will be able to trust God and believe His promises; fear will be pushed out of your life and be taken over by love; thankfulness and praise will become your new language and negativity will fade. You will also become more positive: people will see genuine joy on your face and ask, "What's going on?" Compassion and forgiveness will flow easily.

Let us close with this Scripture:

"Jesus answered and said unto him, If a man love me, he will keep my words: and my Father will love him, and we will come unto him, and make our abode with him."

John 14:23

According to Strong's, "our abode" means, "a staying, i.e., residence (the act or the place)." Webster's Dictionary defines abide as, "to dwell permanently or continuously: occupy a place as one's legal domicile."

Wherever you go, God is with you; so is Jesus and the Holy Spirit. Can you imagine this? You will never have to say that you are lonely again because He lives in you, and you are part of His family!

The Father Loves

Chapter 2

A FATHER OF MERCY AND COMFORT

I have always found that mercy bears richer fruits than strict justice.

-Abraham Lincoln

Where does mercy come from? We picture mothers having mercy, and that is true. But, where did they get it from? The source of mercy comes from God.

"Blessed be God, even the Father of our Lord Jesus Christ, the Father of mercies, and the God of all comfort;[3] who comforteth us in all our tribulation, that we may be able to comfort them which are in any trouble, by the comfort wherewith we ourselves are comforted of God."[4]

2 Corinthians 1:3-4

When I first saw this Scripture, I couldn't believe I was seeing it with my own eyes. Wow. Mercy and comfort come from God the Father. He is a Father, and even encouragement comes from Him. That's what the Bible says. Jesus also called the Holy Spirit, our "Comforter."

Let's read this same Scripture in the Amplified:

"Blessed be the God and Father of our Lord Jesus Christ, the Father of sympathy (pity and mercy) and the God [Who is the Source] of every comfort (consolation and encouragement),[3] Who comforts (consoles and encourages) us in every trouble (calamity and affliction), so that we may also be able to comfort (console and encourage) those who are in any kind of trouble or distress, with the comfort (consolation and encouragement) with which we ourselves are comforted (consoled and encouraged) by God."[4]

These Scriptures will set you free. God is an expert at healing broken hearts. Let's go further to verse 5 in this Scripture, where you will see something interesting:

> *"For the more we suffer for Christ, the more God will shower us with his comfort through Christ."*
>
> **2 Corinthians 1:5 NLT**

This reminds me of all the saints who have been so violently persecuted for Christ's sake; the deeper the suffering, the deeper the comfort. God thought of every provision we would ever need—what a loving Father He is. Those of you who have gone through a divorce as I have, know the hurt. God hurts for us. His Word brings healing to our hearts:

> *"For we do not have a High Priest Who is unable to understand and sympathize and have a shared feeling with our weaknesses and infirmities and liability to the assaults of temptation, but One Who has been tempted in every respect as we are, yet without sinning."*
>
> **Hebrews 4:15 AMP**

Remember, God in the flesh was here on earth for thirty-three years. He understands.

He Has Seen Every One of Your Tears

"You number and record my wanderings; put my tears into Your bottle—are they not in Your book?"

Psalm 56:8, AMP

He speaks about Hezekiah,

"I have heard thy prayer, I have seen thy tears."

Isaiah 38:5

Why would God care about our tears? If you are a parent, you can remember when your kiddos skinned their knees and came running into your arms. Yes, it was comforting for them to have those cute little cartoon bandages, but more than anything, the comfort really came from mom or dad's hug. It is sad to think that not everyone has experienced that warmth as a child. But God sees our tears; He knows all things.

No one knows your heart like God does. He mends and restores your hurts back to wholeness. Come on. Answer God as you hear Him offering comfort and love. The love you can feel is real. Use your imagination, close your eyes and see Him wrapping His fatherly arms around you. Receive it. If you truly do, He promises that you will never, ever be the same. You will feel born again. Because friend, if you do accept His invitation, you are born again.

God Is The Father and Source of Mercy

"ALL the paths of the Lord are mercy and truth unto such as keep his covenant and his testimonies."

Psalm 25:10, emphasis mine

"For I will be merciful to their unrighteousness, and their sins and their iniquities will I remember no more."

Hebrews 8:12

"For we have not an high priest which cannot be touched with the feeling of our infirmities; but was in all points tempted like as we are, yet without sin.[15] Let us

> *therefore come boldly unto the throne of grace, that we may obtain mercy, and find grace to help in time of need."*[16]
>
> *Hebrews 4:15-16*

Imagine a small, remote village in Africa where there is only one well of water for their everyday needs. Each family struggles day after day carrying the buckets, traipsing through the woods, and carring heavy loads from the well. It's the only water source for the whole village. Similarly, your Father God is the source from which ALL MERCY comes from.

A Bike Accident

One sunny afternoon, I was riding my bicycle home from school. I saw a man hurrying to make a right turn; he only looked to his left and didn't see me on his right. When he hit me, it happened so fast that when I looked at the driver, he appeared more frightened than I! My bike got banged up and bent to the point that it was no longer rideable, so I struggled clumsily with it while I walked the long two blocks home. I was fine, a little bruised, but mostly shaken. When I opened the front door, I cried myself right into the arms of my mother.

Now, we know that the Holy Spirit lives in us to comfort and love us, but many times God uses His creation to do the same. Ever remember feeling a soft, gentle breeze caress your face just like a tender kiss? Or a butterfly crossing your path at just that "perfect" moment? The ocean's waves are amazingly calming and refreshing for our soul and a beautiful sunset produces a serenity that mimics eternity's endless love. Here is a comforting Scripture:

"He makes me to lie down in green pastures..."

Psalm 23:2

"Every good gift and every perfect gift is from above, and cometh down from the Father of lights..."

James 1:17

"As one whom his mother comforteth, so will I comfort you."

Isaiah 66:13

"Blessed be the God and Father of our Lord Jesus Christ, which according to his abundant mercy hath begotten us again unto a lively hope by the resurrection of Jesus Christ from the dead,³ to an inheritance incorruptible, and undefiled, and that fadeth not away, reserved in heaven for you,⁴ who are kept by the power of God through faith unto salvation ready to be revealed in the last time."⁵

1 Peter 1:3-5

"For thy mercy is great unto the heavens, and thy truth unto the clouds."

Psalm 57:10

If there were ever a Psalm of mercy, it would be Psalm 103. There are twenty-two verses in this Psalm that speak of His wonderful mercy. I recommend taking some time to fully digest this Scripture for yourself. The following verses do a beautiful job in highlighting His mercy for us.

A Father of Mercy and Comfort

"Bless the Lord, O my soul: and all that is within me, bless his holy name.[1] Bless the Lord, O my soul, and forget not all his benefits:[2] who forgiveth all thine iniquities; who healeth all thy diseases;[3] who redeemeth thy life from destruction; who crowneth thee with lovingkindness and tender mercies;[4] who satisfieth thy mouth with good things; so that thy youth is renewed like the eagle's.[5] The Lord is merciful and gracious, slow to anger, and plenteous in mercy.[8] For as the heaven is high above the earth, so great is his mercy toward them that fear him.[11] As far as the east is from the west, so far hath he removed our transgressions from us.[12] Like as a father pitieth his children, so the Lord pitieth them that fear him.[13] As for man, his days are as grass: as a flower of the field, so he flourisheth."[15]

Psalm 103:1-5,8,11-13,15

God Sent a Father to Help Jesus Carry the Cross

A beautiful example of God's mercy and compassion for us is given in the Gospel of Mark. God sent His One and only Son to save us; He freely gave Him as an offering. This was done on our behalf, even though our Heavenly Father dearly loved his Son, Jesus.

How hard would it be to give up your child for someone else? I don't believe that most of us would. How much more difficult would it be for the God of this universe, Who has always been One with His Son, to give up Jesus for this world?

God watched Jesus go through tremendous suffering; watching and yet not doing anything as if His hands were tied. We know, however, that His hands were not tied; but rather, that the Father, Son, and Holy Spirit chose to endure this together for us. He couldn't be there. Jesus needed comfort and found no earthly help.

A Father of Mercy and Comfort

However, as Jesus was carrying the cross, God provided mercy and comfort through an earthly father, Simon. God anticipated Jesus' needs and provided the help He knew that His son was going to need. Jesus carried the cross in His beaten state to the point where He physically couldn't bear it any longer. Even in the flesh, Jesus still knew (and experienced) the love and compassion of God the Father.

> *"And when they had mocked him, they took off the purple from him, and put his own clothes on him, and led him out to crucify him.*[20] *And they compel one Simon a Cyrenian, who passed by, coming out of the country, the father of Alexander and Rufus, to bear his cross."*[21]
>
> *Mark 15:20-21*

God is so good. He knew His son had to suffer the most excruciating of pains. He gave Him for our sakes, but in His detailed planning, He put this caring man right in the path of Jesus. Simon, a father with a father's heart, just happened to be passing by, coming out of the country.

Simon was in the right place at the right time. The Bible says he was a father of two sons. I wonder if he thought about his boys, 'What if that was my son?' The Word says that They compelled him and They did; Simon chose to help Jesus. You see, we are God's hands, voice, arms, and feet. He loves through us, speaks and touches others through us. We are partners together with Him. He needs us to touch this dying world, for WE are present in this world. Only the heart of a real father, like this man, could do something so selfless in the presence of such barbaric Roman soldiers.

Simon obeyed the voice of God in his heart, as we should. Love doesn't think first and play it safe by not acting. Real love jumps in to save, just as Jesus and Simon did. Both Jesus and Simon expressed their love to their Father by being obedient to Him in their hearts; and by doing so, they proved the Father's love to you and me.

Chapter 3

GOD HAS EMOTIONS

When a father gives to his son, both laugh; when a son gives to his father, both cry.

-Jewish Proverb

How can a person love if they don't have emotions? God has emotions, and we are made in His image.

"Let us make man in our image, after our likeness."

Genesis 1:26

Why do we find it impossible to believe that God is not bereft of emotion? Some of us have never considered whether or not God possesses emotional qualities. We have two eyes, two ears, one mouth, and two arms, just like Him. We cry, we laugh, we get angry, sad, and even passionate. What makes us think that God doesn't possess these emotional qualities, if we are made in His image, and after His likeness? Where do we think emotions come from?

All good things come from God the Father. Can you envision your Father God singing? After all, He is the one who created music; He created all things.

"And God saw every thing that he had made, and, behold, it was very good."

Genesis 1:31

"The Lord thy God in the midst of thee is mighty; he will save, he will rejoice over thee with joy; he will rest in his love, he will joy over thee with **singing.**"

Zephaniah 3:17, emphasis mine

I can't wait to hear God sing! He rejoices over you with joy and rejoices over you with singing! We never picture God smiling, but He is the source of all joy. The thought of you and I brings Him much pleasure, not sorrow. Even in the midst of our sin. He is the One who made recompense for our sins and He has no regrets about how He has made you. He rejoices over you with joy…pure joy.

A Picture of Your Heavenly Father

The true heart of the Father for us reminds me of the story of the Prodigal Son. This is an example of the Father's love and mercy towards us. You can read the story in Luke 15:11-32. After the shame and disgrace that his son brought to him through his rebellious actions; this father had every right to disown him.. But each day the father was waiting for him to come back home, and when he finally decided to come back, his father was still waiting for him with great expectation. Read as we pick up here in verse 20:

> *"So he got up and came to his [own] father. But while he was still a long way off, his father saw him and was moved with pity and tenderness [for him]; and he ran and embraced him and kissed him [fervently]"*[20] *But the father said to his bond servants, Bring quickly the best robe (the festive robe of honor) and put it on him; and give him a ring for his hand and sandals for his feet.*[22] *And bring out that [wheat-]fattened calf and kill it; and let us revel and*

> *feast and be happy and make merry,*[23] *Because this my son was dead and is alive again; he was lost and is found! And they began to revel and feast and make merry."*[24]
>
> *Luke 15:20,22-24, AMP*

Many of us have heard this story before. But now, let us put on their shoes…imagine yourself as the Prodigal Son, and God as the father from this story. The Prodigal Son is a portrayal of what our Father's heart is really like when we turn away from him. He is patiently waiting for us, and is well-ready to embrace us as His own. An earthly parent would be weeping—what makes us think that God our Father would be any different? If a person was lost, and comes to know Jesus as their Savior, they are saved. The angels rejoice when one comes to the Kingdom of God. So, let's just think about what God's response is: picture Him clapping His hands with excitement, and rejoicing over you when you come home.

A Runaway Teen

I have a personal testimony similar to that of the Prodigal Son. In 9th grade I tried to fit in the crowd so much that I started to hang out with the wrong people. My friends did not truly accept me and I was blinded from the truth. My parents cared about me, but were unwilling to let me go to parties with these "trouble-makers." So, it was not long before I decided to run away from home—what a horrible experience that was. I quickly saw my friends for who they really were. Looking back, I see that I gave my parents lots of grief when I was a teenager.

It is embarrassing for me when I recall these events in my life. However, I believe that it will bless someone who needs to hear my story… It was very early in the morning (on a weekend) that I went from house to house to find somewhere to stay with a friend. No one would help me because they did not want to risk getting into trouble with the police.

Finally, on the last morning, one of my friends' mothers took me in and fed me and let me take a bath. When I walked out of the bathroom, my mother was sitting there waiting for me, crying and asking me to please, come home. At first, I felt betrayed by my friend's mother; and yet, in that moment, there was silence and peace within me concerning her. I also had a repentant heart heavy with humility and shame on account of what I had done. What could I say? So, my mother took us to a park near our house.

When we got out of the car and got comfortable sitting down on the grass, she turned to me and asked, "What is it you want, Linda?" I was honestly too young and confused to know exactly what I wanted. Back then, I just wanted to belong. I wanted to be accepted, to feel special, and to be loved. At that time in my life, I was attending a very strict private school. I hated it. It was a new school for me, and I did not know very many people. "Mom, can I just go to a normal high school close to home, where I can make some new friends?"

She calmly replied, "Yes, you can." Then she hugged me, no questions asked. We both cried at that moment. My mother really listened to me. She loved and truly cared enough for me to come and get me—to come and find me. She and my dad, who was waiting for me at home, both forgave me and welcomed me home again with open arms. I can relate to the story of the Prodigal Son because I know what it's like to be welcomed back when you know you don't deserve it. To be freely forgiven. This is freedom.

God Is Joyful

*"The Lord is merciful and gracious, **slow to anger**, and plenteous in mercy.*

Psalm 103:8, emphasis mine

The Lord is slow to anger, which means He is plenteous in mercy. I don't know about you, but I'll take the plenteous in mercy because I have taken many opportunities to disappoint God. There is joy on the other side of anger. This is who He is and who He will always be when/if we fall on our face and flat out fail, we can always look for God's love when we need Him.

1 John 3:20 says, "For if our heart condemn us, God is greater than our heart, and knoweth all things." God is full of joy and is rich in mercy towards us. All we need to do is draw near to

Him This begs the question: how do we begin to draw near to him when we don't feel accepted—when "our hearts condemn us?"

> *"But without faith it is impossible to **please** him: for he that cometh to God must believe that he is, and that he is a rewarder of them that diligently seek him."*
>
> **Hebrews 11:6, emphasis mine**

The word "pleased" in Hebrew is, "to be well-pleased" (Strong's #2100). If that is not joy, please tell me what is. If you are like many people, a joyful God is not quite the picture you have been brought up to see, especially when you feel like He is mad at you. We must turn our thinking around, and see Him as He really is. He is a God of love; a real Father who is merciful and full of joy.

> *"Thou wilt shew me the path of life: in thy presence is fulness of joy; at thy right hand there are pleasures for evermore."*
>
> **Psalm 16:11**

Indeed, God has emotions, and we are made in His image. He gets hurt and sad, just like we do. What makes

God sad? If believing Him and His word pleases Him, as in Hebrews 11:6, then doubting and distrusting Him displeases Him. When someone doesn't trust you, what happens? You become disappointed because your good intentions are not valued or they are misconstrued. You might think that because God is perfect, He doesn't have any feelings. That isn't true because "robot" is not part of His character. He gave us emotions to express, just like He has emotions to express.

God's Emotions Are Stable

Now, even though we're talking about God having feelings, an important fact must be brought to light. God does not live, nor is led by His feelings. God lives by faith. Many people on this earth are led by their feelings. God is the opposite; He lives by faith and anyone who chooses to relate to Him must come to His level.

Unless you live by faith, you will not be able to relate to God. God is a Spirit (John 4:24), and if you want to commune with Him, it must be done in Spirit, and by faith. Feelings are in the realm of the physical. The physical and the spiritual are two very different worlds. Faith sees things in the spiritual sense, while feelings and emotions respond to the natural and are of the flesh. They are separate from the Spirit. You can be living out of your emotions without really knowing God, and still be saved. But until you choose to live in the Spirit, you will be living differently than God does; following after your emotions, and only believing what you see.

If you are led and respond by your feelings and God is led and responds by faith, this type of relationship dynamic would be like a fish trying to make friends with a bird. The fish swims all day and lives and breathes in the water; that is his world. The bird flies through the air with the greatest of ease and pulls his slimy worms out of the ground for breakfast. What could these two possibly have in common? They live in two very different worlds. If the fish wanted to get to know the bird, then he would have to grow some feathers and breathe air like he breathes. We can't expect to know God until we become familiar with His language and His ways.

Thankfully, unlike the fish, we CAN know God. First, we must receive the finished work of Jesus on the cross and believe that He died for us. Then we will be born with a new spirit and we will have God's Spirit in us. "But ye are not in the flesh, but in the Spirit, if so be that the Spirit of God dwell in you" (Romans 8:9).

What pleases God? Faith. If you live by faith, God is pleased with you. He is proud of you. "But without faith it is impossible to please him: for he that cometh to God must believe that he is, and that he is a rewarder of them that diligently seek him" (Hebrews 11:6).

Sometimes we make mistakes and think we've heard God. We head in a particular direction later realizing that we weren't hearing God at all. I have done something like this before and it can be very disappointing. Personally, I felt as though I "missed" it. Failed. God, on the other hand, sees this quite differently. He is pleased that you put your faith in Him and followed your heart. A heart willing to follow Him. "For if our heart condemns us, God is greater than our heart and knoweth all things" (1 John 3:20).

Imagine yourself taking a detour. You may be on a detour, but your Father will always get you back on the right track; all you have to do is trust Him. God has always made provision for our failures, just like a good parent does. We must "[be] confident of this very thing, that he which hath begun a good work in you will perform it until the day of Jesus Christ" (Philippians 1:6).

The only way for us to be confident in this hope is to remember that God will finish what He started in us and we must continue to live by faith. This Scripture is quoted in the Bible in four different places: "The Just shall live by faith" (Romans 1:17, Hebrews 10:38, Galatians 3:11, and Habakkuk 2:4).

Notice in Habakkuk 2:4 it states, "The just shall live by *his* faith." This Scripture further confirms that what Jesus started in you, He will also finish. Even Jesus lived by faith for the hope that was set before Him, which was us.

As believers, we *live* by faith in Jesus. We do not just practice faith every now and then on Sundays, or when we attend special conferences. It is a lifestyle, not a formula.

> *"Now the just shall live by faith: but if any man draw back, my soul shall have no pleasure in him."*
>
> ***Hebrews 10:38***

We could say that living by faith is also trusting God and believing that His promises are for us. It is up to us to decide to have faith in Jesus and all He has for us. And, when we do, we know that God takes great pleasure in us.

Why Do We Have Feelings?

God gave us feelings for a purpose. For example, we can feel the beauty of the creation He has made for us, which might illicit many different responses in every one of us, such as thankfulness or joy. When we praise and sing to Him, we can feel His majesty, and sense His tender love in our hearts. Sometimes, we have feelings of mercy or compassion towards others. With feelings, we often respond by letting God's love flow through our hearts towards others.

Feelings are not bad, but we should not allow ourselves to be led by them. They can be so wishy-washy. The reason we cannot depend on them is because they are not based on facts and, consequently tend to lead people astray. We live by emotions way too much.

For example, if you wake up in the morning feeling sad, and you continue to dwell on this sad feeling, the rest of your day could go downhill. Think of your emotions as ocean waves; they go back and forth, continuously being dictated by the wind and weather changes.

Now-a-days, many of us live by our emotions. In fact, many people let their feelings guide their lives and allow them to be the basis for decision-making. You might find some people saying, "But this is how I feel, and I can't help it." But, we can put a stop to this pattern because God never changes. He is a rock; steadfast, immovable, and un-changeable! We can count on Him and His faithfulness.

> *"Jesus Christ the same yesterday, and to day, and for ever."*
>
> *Hebrews 13:8*

> *"Every good gift and every perfect gift is from above, and cometh down from the Father of lights, with whom is no variableness, neither shadow of turning."*
>
> *James 1:17*

"For I am the Lord, I change not…"

Malachi 3:6

Being Led By Your Feelings

What does a day of being led by your feelings look like? Let us imagine Betty, a single career-woman, who just woke up and is now in the process of getting ready for the day. She cuts herself shaving, and lets out a small shriek, "Agh! That hurt!" Then, as she goes to make her breakfast, she burns the toast and the bacon. "No way… no time to make more," she grumbles.

Rushing to the car, Betty finds out that she has a flat tire. Out of anger and frustration, she raves, "Oh, wow, this is going to be a lousy day!" From then on, Betty allows her frustrations to affect her, grouchily complaining about them all day to whoever will listen.

That is a pretty accurate picture of someone's day being led by their emotions and circumstances. They are a victim in everyone's path; at least, that's how they see themselves.

Does that sound like anyone you have ever met before? Sometimes, they even try to outdo one another by arguing about who had the worst day! "Well, let me tell you about what happened to me today…" they exclaim!

Being Led By the Word of God

You wake up in the morning and start thanking the Lord for His new mercies and favor, and for His lovingkindness. While getting ready for the day, you cut yourself shaving and say, "Body, the word of God says you are blessed, so be healed." Then you make breakfast and happen to burn the toast and the bacon. "No matter, Lord, thank You that I have lunch; it won't hurt me to do without breakfast this morning."

You go to your car, and find out you have a flat tire. "Lord, I give you this problem, and I thank you for working it all out. Thank you that I have Road Service, who I can call to come and fix it. Praise God! While I wait, I'll go and make some more toast and bacon."

Going to work, you sing praises to Him, not worrying about one thing. As soon as you walk in, someone says, "You're late, how's it going?" You say, "Oh, it was just a flat tire, no problem at all. Hey, you look great in that color!"

This was the same scenario with different outlooks and different responses. A man of faith does not let his circumstances move him. He moves his circumstances with God's word and His ways. Our feelings may fluctuate, our circumstances may change, and times may change; but, God's Word never changes. We can hold on to His wonderful, steadfast promises! Give in to His Word and live your life by faith.

If we want to please God and make Him happy, we can live by faith. One way to do this is by believing in His Word. When we believe His Word, we show God that we love Him because we trust in what He says. You will find that He is faithful, and is worthy of all your love and devotion. He is good, and His mercy endures forever!

Choosing to live by the Word of God is achievable, just as choosing not to live by your feelings is achievable. The Word changes you and your outlook on life; you become positive because the Word is positive. Don't let your feelings ruin your life; let the Word of God change your life! Praise our God, Jehovah!

Chapter 4

OUR FATHER SEES AND HEARS US

A friend is a person with whom I may be sincere. Before him I may think aloud.

-Ralph Waldo Emerson

What are some of the things God is doing in heaven right now? When I reflected upon this question, I thought about myself as a parent, and took a look at the sweet relationships I have with my children. If you have kids, try and do the same. If you don't have kids, look at the relationships you have with your parents, or with people that you love and care about.

Earthly Family & Heavenly Family

When you are a parent, think of how much your kids occupy your mind. You love them so much, you want what is best for them, and you try to anticipate their needs. You plan for them, excited to bring surprises at times. You go to sleep praying for each one. When they hurt, you hurt more. Why isn't it true that you sometimes wish you could take their place, if it could spare them any pain? Or, if they receive a gift, it is the same as you receiving a gift.

I remember one Christmas, when they were small, their dad and I gave them their first bikes. We assembled and parked them in front of the tree. One of us woke the kids up and the other was waiting with the camera to catch the surprised look on their faces. They were still half asleep as they saw their new bikes; we were the ones feeling excited. They got excited later! Another time, I remember building a two-story doll house out of a kit for my daughter when she was about 5 years old for Christmas. Making and buying miniature furniture and curtains; painting the house pink. I would wait till she went to bed each night to work on it. I will never forget the delighted look on her face! But even before I saw that look, I would often think about the first moment she would see it.

If God is a Father (and our heavenly Father at that), why should He be any different? Think about this thought for a moment: If God SO LOVED the world, that He gave HIS ONLY SON, that whosoever believed in Him, would never perish, but live eternally…if God gave His most precious and valuable possession…then there must have been something He wanted even more. US.

When you offer a gift, it isn't yours any longer. Certainly, God knew that when He gave us Jesus, it was only for a time, that He would get His precious Son back, but nonetheless, He did let go. The act of giving is to let go. But, He also gave in hopes of getting us back.

When you really want something, all you do is think about it. God thinks about you, desiring a friendship with you, spending time with you, enjoying you and you enjoying Him. This means that you are on His heart. He wants to protect and care for you, provide and treasure you, defend and surprise you. Doesn't that sound just like the relationship you have with your children?

If you have made Jesus your Lord and Savior, you are in Christ; and because of Christ, He sees and hears you and watches over you "because as Christ is, so are you in this world" (1 John 4:17). You see, this means you have the same favor as

Jesus; you have the same blessings as Jesus. That is a huge statement to swallow. This is part of the New Covenant! He is looking forward to you responding willingly and freely to Him as your Father. The thought of having this relationship for eternity is so awesome, it is almost beyond comprehension!

He's Watching You With Love

"Blessed is the nation whose God is the Lord; and the people whom he hath chosen for his own inheritance."[12] *The Lord looketh from heaven; he beholdeth all the sons of men."*[13] *From the place of his habitation he looketh upon all the inhabitants of the earth."*[14]

Psalm 33:12-14

Now, let's investigate further into this verse. Verses 12 and 13 are speaking about us as His children, His inheritance (estate, portion, possession). Verse 14 is speaking about all the rest of those who are not His own. Those that do not know Him or have not believed in His Son, Jesus.

Verse 13:

The Lord looks/ Nabat: *To scan, look intently, regard with pleasure, favor, care, consider (Strong's #5027).*

He sees/ Raa: *To behold, consider, gaze, approve, be near, enjoy, have experience, take heed, mark, meet, perceive, present, provide, regard, respect, stare, think, view (Strong's #7200).*

All the sons of men: *We know this is speaking of his children because the beginning of verse 12 tells us, "blessed is the nation whose God is the Lord."*

Verse 14:

He looks/ Shagach: *Look, peep, glance sharply on all the inhabitants of the earth (Strong's #7688). This is a different Hebrew word; He doesn't look at all the rest of the world same- it's with a sharp glance. Yes, He loves them and He gave His Son for them, even in their sin. But, because they are* *walking in evil and do not have His spirit alive within them, He does not behold them the same.*

Verse 18:

Behold the eye/ Ayin: *a fountain, countenance, eyebrow, outward appearance (Strong's #5869).*

There are several Scriptures that speak of God seeing us:

"For the righteous Lord loveth righteousness; his countenance doth behold the upright."

Psalm 11:7

"He that keepeth thee will not slumber."

Psalm 121:3

"I will instruct thee and teach thee in the way which thou shalt go: I will guide thee with mine eye."

Psalm 32:8

> *"The face of the Lord is against them that do evil, to cut off the remembrance of them from the earth."*
>
> **Psalm 34:16**

In the story about Hagar, Sarai's maid, who fled from Sarai while being pregnant with Ishmael, the angel of the Lord appeared unto her. The angel gave Hagar a message, and encouraged her to go back:

> *"And she called the name of the Lord that spake unto her, Thou God seest me."*
>
> **Genesis 16:13**

El Roi: God sees. Here, Hagar referred to one of the mighty names of God.

"Remembering without ceasing your work of faith, and labour of love, and patience of hope in our Lord Jesus Christ, in the sight of God and our Father."

1 Thessalonians 1:3

> *"That thine alms may be in secret: and thy Father which seeth in secret himself shall reward thee openly."*
>
> *Matthew 6:4*

This idea alone should persuade you to want to please Him, and do right in His sight-knowing that He sees all you do. This is a very humbling thought, indeed.

Remember when we talked in the last chapter about His emotions? Well, now we speak of some of His senses. We see, touch, smell and hear. Where did we get these from? Who had them first? Whose image are we made in, and from whose likeness have we been created? God the Father also created smells because He, too, is able to smell.

> *"And the Lord smelled a sweet savour; and the Lord said in his heart…"*
>
> *Genesis 8:21*

> *"An odour of a sweet smell, a sacrifice acceptable, well-pleasing to God."*
>
> *Philippians 4:18*

Think of all of the wonderful, fragrant smells on this earth. It is He that thought of each one's unique smell. Do you have some favorite fragrances? This is just one of the many ways that He loves to pleasure us with His gifts.

The Father Hears You

He sees us. He smells our offerings of love as sweet fragrances to Him. He also hears us with His own ears:

"Lord, thou hast heard the desire of the humble: thou wilt prepare their heart, thou wilt cause thine ear to hear."

Psalm 10:17

"In my distress I called upon the Lord, and cried unto my God: he heard my voice out of his temple, and my cry came before him, even into his ears."

Psalm 18:6

"The Lord hear thee in the day of trouble; the name of the God of Jacob defend thee."

Psalm 20:1

"I sought the Lord, and he heard me, and delivered me from all my fears.[4] The righteous cry, and the Lord heareth, and delivereth them out of all their troubles."[17]

Psalm 34:4,17

Jesus knew that His Father heard Him:

"Then they took away the stone from the place where the dead was laid. And Jesus lifted up his eyes, and said, Father, I thank thee that thou hast heard me.[41] And I knew that thou hearest me always."[42]

John 11:41-42

Many times in our lives, we think God doesn't hear us. We have believed religion and the traditions of men. If you are a child of God, and believe that Jesus died for you, was buried and rose again, and lives at the right hand of the Father, then you have every right to be heard by God. If you don't know God as your

Father, you can know Him! He would love for you to know Him. I welcome you to pray the prayer in the very last chapter of this book. You can know Him today.

> *"For we have not an high priest which cannot be touched with the feeling of our infirmities; but was in all points tempted like as we are, yet without sin.[15] Let us therefore come **boldly** unto the throne of grace, that we may obtain mercy, and find grace to help in time of need."[16]*
>
> ***Hebrews 4:15-16, emphasis mine***

The Greek definition for the word "Boldly" is, "with confidence, openly." What does this mean to you? Do you think we would boldly come to the throne of God, and just stand there and do nothing? When we come to Him in prayer, He is listening!

Just as your child comes to you freely and asks you for lunch money or new shoes, do you tell them, "Dare you come and ask such a thing?" No, quite the opposite. Most likely, we would say, "What kind do you want?" or "Wait til payday Honey." How much more does your Heavenly Father want to listen to you, and hear about your needs? He owns the cattle on a thousand hills!

He longs for you to come to Him instead of you trying to fix things on your own, and trying to meet your own needs. We have things so backwards. He hears us. He longs for you to call upon Him. He would love for you to speak to Him. Are you longing to hear from Him?

Sometimes we are too busy with our own plans and agendas, or we are too busy telling Him about our problems, that we forget to just be still, worship, wait, and listen. We can be like the husband who is reading his morning paper, nodding, "Hmmmm…yes, Dear, of course, Dear," while his wife is trying to get his attention. Or, like the Dad who is trying to visit with his kids, who are mesmerized by the TV, computer games and MP3 players.

Read the following verses from Psalm 81, and see how much God wants you to hear from Him. Here He is speaking to Israel in their rebelliousness. To hear His heart for them is very enlightening.

"For this is a statute for Israel, an ordinance of the God of Jacob.⁴ This He ordained in Joseph [the savior] for a testimony when He went out over the land of Egypt. The speech of One Whom I knew not did I hear [saying],⁵ I removed his shoulder from the burden; his hands were freed from the basket.⁶ You called in distress and I delivered you; I answered you in the secret place of thunder; I tested you at the waters of Meribah. Selah [pause, and calmly think of that]!⁷ Hear, O My people, and I will admonish you—O Israel, if you would listen to Me!⁸ There shall no strange god be among you, neither shall you worship any alien god.⁹ I am the Lord your God, Who brought you up out of the land of Egypt. Open your mouth wide and I will fill it.¹⁰ But My people would not hearken to My voice, and Israel would have none of Me.¹¹ So I gave them up to their own hearts' lust and let them go after their own stubborn will, that they might follow their own counsels.¹² Oh, that My people would listen to Me, that Israel would walk in My ways!¹³ Speedily then I would subdue their enemies and turn My hand against their adversaries.¹⁴ [Had Israel

> *listened to Me in Egypt, then] those who hated the Lord would have come cringing before Him, and their defeat would have lasted forever.*[15] *[God] would feed [Israel now] also with the finest of the wheat; and with honey out of the rock would I satisfy you."*[16]

> **Psalm 81:4-16, AMP**

It is incredible how the God of the universe yearns for a relationship with you and me! He would rather spend time with His children than anything else, because that's what good fathers do. Good fathers want the absolute best always for their kids. They want to protect them from all harm. They want to see them succeed in all that they do.

We must keep reminding ourselves that a healthy relationship takes two voices, two pairs of eyes and ears, and two hearts. When you come, worship and sing to Him, and thank Him for His goodness and His word. Then, sit and take some time to talk to Him, knowing that He's a good Father who cares. Listen, and let Him tell you how much He dearly loves you.

Chapter 5

THE FATHER KNOWS ALL ABOUT YOU

My best friend is the one who brings out the best in me.

-Henry Ford

Only a husband and wife who have really known each other a long time, best friends, or even a close family member can say, "Oh, I know you. I know exactly what you are going to say, and how you will respond." Because of the history and memories you have shared together, they feel they know you. Those who are closest to you may know a lot about you, but who really knows you? Who knows the deepest secrets and longings of you heart? The Father does.

"For He knoweth the secrets of the heart."

Psalm 44:21

After all, He was there when you were conceived. Psalm 139 has a wealth of information about how God knows you. You may have read this Psalm a million times, but let's ponder it. The word "Know" is used 5 times. In Hebrew it means, "Yada." This word is also used for an intimate acquaintance (Strong's #3045). For example:

> "And the Lord said unto Moses, I will do this thing also that thou hast spoken: for thou hast found grace in my sight, and I know thee by name."
>
> ***Exodus 33:17***

> "O Lord, thou hast searched me, and known me.[1] Thou knowest my downsitting and mine uprising, thou understandest my thought afar off.[2] Thou compassest my path and my lying down, and art acquainted with all my ways."[3]
>
> ***Psalm 139:1-3***

He Created You Inside and Out

"For thou hast possessed my reins: thou hast covered me in my mother's womb.[13] I will praise thee; for I am fearfully and wonderfully made."[14]

Psalm 139:13-14

Can you imagine? We see sonograms of babies still in their mother's tummies on social media websites. We see the little head, and how it's positioned. But God the Father was there. God the Father made it happen.

The next verse in the Amplified states:

"My frame was not hidden from you when I was being formed in secret and intricately and curiously wrought as if embroidered with various colors in the depths of the earth a region of darkness and mystery."

Psalm 139:15

He knew you even before you were formed, with all of your days written in His book.

"Thine eyes did see my substance, yet being unperfect; and in thy book all my members were written, which in continuance were fashioned, when as yet there was none of them."

Psalm 139:16

He Knows All of Your Days

Take the life of an average person who lives until they are 70 years old. His days on this earth would equal about 25,550 (plus 9 months in the womb). God saw every one of those days before the baby was ever formed; then, when it was being formed, He was there to see it. Think of that. Your first words, your first day of kindergarten, the day you walked down the aisle to get married, He remembers. Every single word you have ever said, and every word you will ever say again in your whole life is known to Him. God knows and cares about every detail of your life.

"For there is not a word in my tongue, but, lo, O Lord, thou knowest it altogether."

Psalm 139:4

According to an online article by Nikhil Swaminathan in <u>Scientific American,</u> research was done by collecting data from 396 university students, 210 women and 186 men, at colleges in Texas, Arizona and Mexico. They estimated the total number of words that each volunteer spoke daily, assuming that they were awake at least 17 to 24 hours.

In most of the samples, the average number of words spoken by men and women were about the same; women at 16,215 words and men at 15,669. Various research has been done, and data may vary from one extreme to the other. Some studies say women speak more than men. Regardless of how many words you speak in a day, your Father God knows every one of them. Can you imagine a lifetime of words?

He Has Knowledge of Every Living Being

He knows about all things. Let us think further outside the box...what about the birds? Some of us may not pay a lot of attention to them, besides throwing a few french fries out to them while eating outside a fast-food restaurant, but we rarely ever give them a second thought. Well, God the merciful Father, is quite the opposite. He pays close attention to all of His creation:

> *"What is the price of two sparrows—one copper coin? But not a single sparrow can fall to the ground without your Father knowing it.[29] And the very hairs on your head are all numbered.[30] So don't be afraid; you are more valuable to God than a whole flock of sparrows."[31]*
>
> *Matthew 10:29-31, NLT*

> *"For every beast of the forest is mine, and the cattle upon a thousand hills.[10] I know all the fowls of the mountains: and the wild beasts of the field are mine…[11] the world is mine, and the fulness thereof."[12]*
>
> *Psalm 50:10-12*

How can any one of us think that God doesn't care?

Security Belongs to Us

As a child growing up in a middle class family in Southern California, I didn't need to worry about the bare necessities in life, such as having enough good food to eat or clothes to wear. It was our tradition to have a birthday party complete with a special home-made cake, colorfully wrapped presents and relatives! My mouth waters, just thinking about my favorite birthday cake smothered with rich chocolate cream cheese frosting, covered with walnuts.

When children know they are loved and taken care of, they don't worry about day to day needs, or even future wants. They are secure in love. This is an ideal situation. I know that many children are not well-taken care of, but forgotten and even abused. I'm sure it is heart-breaking to our Father, Who sent His Son, Jesus, according to John 10:10, to give us abundant life. We as Christians must remember to depend on our loving Father, and to trust and believe that He knows all things, and that He has a well-thought-out plan for us.

Jesus speaks to his disciples:

"Take no thought for your life, what ye shall eat; neither for the body, what ye shall put on.[22] The life is more than meat, and the body is more than raiment.[23] Consider the ravens: for they neither sow nor reap; which neither have storehouse nor barn; and God feedeth them: how much more are ye better than the fowls?[24] And which of you with taking thought can add to his stature one cubit?[25] If ye then be not able to do that thing which is least, why take ye thought for the rest?[26] Consider the lilies how they grow: they toil not, they spin not; and yet I say unto you, that Solomon in all his glory was not arrayed like one of these.[27] If then God so clothe the grass, which is to day in the field, and to morrow is cast into the oven; how much more will he clothe you, O ye of little faith?[28] And seek not ye what ye shall eat, or what ye shall drink, neither be ye of doubtful mind.[29] For all these things do the nations of the world seek after: and your Father knoweth that ye have need of these things.[30] But rather seek ye the kingdom of God;

and all these things shall be added unto you.[31] *Fear not, little flock; for it is your Father's good pleasure to give you the kingdom."*[32]

Luke 12:22-32

God is all-knowing and omnipotent. He knows ALL THINGS. He is the only One Who knows the day of the Second Coming of Jesus (Matthew 24:36). It brings such a secure feeling to be able to rest in His care for your future. He knows you, and has provided everything you need to have a good future for you and your family.

The Father Loves

Chapter 6

RELATIONSHIP? BUT I CAN'T SEE HIM...

Have faith in God, God has faith in you.

-Edward Louis Cole

Not just once does the Bible say, "The just shall live by faith." Actually, it is said four times (Habakkuk 2:4, Romans 1:17, Galatians 3:11, Hebrews 10:38). He is trying to get this point across. Also, Hebrews 11:6 says, "It is faith that pleases God." We could then say the opposite, that fear and doubt does not please God. So many times in the Gospels, Jesus said, "Do not be afraid, only believe." Doubt doesn't get any results.

> *"Now the just shall live by faith: but if any man draw back, my soul shall have no pleasure in him."*
>
> ***Hebrews 10:38***

> *"And I heard a great voice out of heaven saying, Behold, the tabernacle of God is with men, and he will dwell with them, and they shall be his people, and God himself shall be with them, and be their God.³ And God shall wipe away all tears from their eyes; and there shall be no more death, neither sorrow, nor crying, neither shall there be any more pain: for the former things are passed away."*⁴
>
> *Revelation 21:3-4*

Glory to God! We must live by faith and believe that He is there for us. He sees whatever we do, hears whatever we say, and knows whatever we think; all before it ever happens. His presence is in you and all around you. Jesus told doubting Thomas, "Blessed are they that have not seen and yet have believed" (John 20:29).

Please Him by trusting in His Word, and stop looking for signs. Remember that His Word is bread and life to you. Once you understand and believe this truth, you won't be able to live without it. I must have the Word of God to exist. Without it, I would die; His Word is LIFE. After you trust that His presence is with you, begin to look inward and listen.

"My sheep hear my voice, and I know them, and they follow me."

John 10:27

"Be still, and know that I am God."

Psalm 46:10

Sometimes, we're so wrapped up in our own needs and prayers. We plead for God's wisdom. Do we even expect a response?

We need to trust that our Father will speak to us, and wait patiently for His calming, comforting answers. In this age of distractions, ear buds, laptops, Internet, and movies, we're over-stimulated. The thought of a complete stop doesn't even appeal to us anymore. Maybe we haven't considered that God would want to talk to us. "Surely, He is too busy running the universe," or "my life is not important," you might think. Well, you are wrong, my friend. God is omnipresent—how could His children be of no importance to Him?

Remember, that good parents are always thinking about their children. They plan, make provision for them, and want the absolute best for them.

You and I Are His Favorite

"God is no respecter of persons."

Acts 10:34

This means He does not play favorites, but loves every person the same. This means that no matter who you are or what you look like, He loves and values you. No matter where you live or what part of the country you live in, He sees you, and you matter to him. Do not let this Earth's "destructor" con you into thinking that you are not greatly valued by your Heavenly Father. He cares about your life right now, right where you are, and His love for you will never fade.

There are only two types of human beings: believers and unbelievers. We are either in darkness or in the light. Which side are you on right now? Which side do you want to be on?

His hand is reaching out to you, calling for you and believing that you will come to Him. He cannot wait for you to answer so that you can live the life He wishes for you to experience. Romans 5:8 speaks of how God showed His love to us in that, "While we were yet sinners, Christ died for us."

In the world in which we live, the most intelligent, talented, famous and beautiful people are treated better than the less-fortunate or uneducated. But, in God's kingdom, the rules are quite different. The Word of God tells us that God cares deeply for the stranger, widowed and fatherless.

> *"A father of the fatherless, and a judge of the widows, is God in his holy habitation.[5] God setteth the solitary in families: he bringeth out those which are bound with chains: but the rebellious dwell in a dry land."[6]*
>
> **Psalm 68:5-6**

Our Heavenly Father is compassionate, and He has promised a special reward for each one of us according to our faithful service and obedience to Him. We serve a merciful God Who never lets any of our kind acts go unnoticed.

Our Comforter

Let us take a look for a moment at the role of the Holy Spirit, which is God's Spirit that lives in us. Jesus left this earth, and is seated at the right hand of God the Father, but He didn't leave us alone. I don't fully understand The Trinity, but this verse is in the same chapter as John 14:26, where Jesus tells us that He is sending the Comforter.

> *"Jesus answered and said unto him, If a man love me, he will keep my words: and my Father will love him, and we will come unto him, and make our abode with him."*
>
> ***John 14:23***

"Abode" is the Greek word, "Mone," which means a staying, residence, abode, mansion (Strong's #3438). This is talking about The Trinity. The Holy Spirit teaches us, guides and comforts us (John 15:26, John 16:13). You can pray in tongues and listen to His wisdom; you can listen to His encouragement and love. Do you need love and encouragement today? Go to Him first, the Father of Comfort; not to men. Go to God! He is the source for all your needs. He is your Shepherd.

When in the natural you have a relationship, it takes time to nurture it, and it takes time for both of you to make memories together. "Koinonia" is the word for fellowship:

> *"God is faithful, by whom ye were called unto the fellowship of his son Jesus Christ our Lord."*
>
> **1 Corinthians 1:9**

The Greek word "Koinonia" comes from the root word, "Koinonos," meaning "partnership, participation, social intercourse, communicate, communion" (Strong's #2844). It's the same word in Acts 2:42: "And they continued steadfastly in the apostles; doctrine and fellowship and in breaking of bread, and in prayers."

Visiting with my family in California for birthdays and holidays is so much richer now that we are Christians. Beautiful fellowship and laughter with family, and enjoying my mother's delicious food. We play our guitars as my brother and my son boldly lead songs of worship. What a blessing!

The Father Loves

Think of precious memories that you have with family or close friends, and although you may not see each other for long periods, doesn't it seem as though time stands still when you get together? These relationships have required us to be interactive; memories have been built together.

It is the same with God the Father, Jesus, and the Holy Spirit; He wants to fellowship with us. Don't let it be one-sided. Let him speak, and actively listen. If we seriously want a meaningful relationship with our Father, we must practice coming to Him daily. Soon He will be a vital part of your life and you will feel Him with you at all times; in all places. You will be able to hear your Father in a crowded, noisy room!

As a young Christian, I was hungry to hear God's voice, but I thought I had to be completely alone, without a soul in sight. I can think of a comical experience of mine while I was visiting Huntington Gardens in Los Angeles, CA. My desire was to meet with God among the beautiful rose and herb gardens without distraction. Picture this: Bible in hand with my sunglasses on, I was ditching people left and right, lurking in the shadows behind bushes, trying to avoid people. It's a wonder why someone didn't call security! This is a good example of trying to mix the physical world with the spiritual without understanding. I didn't know how to hear Him in the spirit. Later, I found out that I could hear God's voice anytime, anywhere. As we grow in God spiritually, we each have our own funny stories to tell!

Use Your Imagination

God gave us an imagination to use. Picture His promises in your life, how it feels, seeing yourself as if you have already obtained it.

> *"Let us therefore come boldly unto the throne of grace, that we may obtain mercy, and find grace to help in time of need."*
>
> ***Hebrews 4:16***

If you would, imagine yourself coming boldly to the Throne of Grace. Picture your loving Father, smiling, waiting to welcome you with eyes of love and compassion, anxious to talk to you. You have a need that you are anxious to discuss with Him. As you talk with your Father for a while, He says, "Child, I'll take care of it for you."

"Thou wilt keep him in perfect peace, whose mind is stayed on thee: because he trusteth in thee."

Isaiah 26:3

"O Lord God of Abraham, Isaac, and of Israel, our fathers, keep this for ever in the imagination of the thoughts of the heart of thy people, and prepare their heart unto thee."

1 Chronicles 29:18

These two highlighted words, "Mind" and "Imagination," come from the Hebrew word, Yeser – "A form, conception, frame, imagination" (Strong's #3336).

You see, we use our imagination every day. You can fix your thoughts on something negative, like worry or fear, or you can think in a positive way, being thankful for God and His word. It is your choice—either way, you are building a framework; a stronghold. God made us with imaginations and we are experts at using them, although many of us focus on negative things.

When we allow ourselves to imagine "worst-case" scenarios and dwell on negative situations long enough, all kinds of strongholds can be built. We dwell on the bills not being paid and let our imaginations run wild, picturing the absolute worst scenarios. That's how strongholds are built. If you think negatively long enough, you can go into deep depression. So, why not turn it around and meditate on God's word and on the things that are above?

I believe God gave us our imagination to help us to meditate, so in turn we could plant His Word deep into our hearts. God's Word is good seed. Imagine being with our heavenly Father, and what the throne of grace looks like; a golden glow of His glory and wonder. Sparkling beauty is all around, like nothing you've ever seen—angels singing sweetly, and the sounds and melodies of heaven are overwhelming; they enrapture your soul. All your senses are engaged. The sweet smells and rich, radiant colors are like nothing you've ever experienced. It is here you find grace to help you. It's here you find mercy. It's here you find total acceptance, no judgment—only love. Just unconditional agape love.

Take a verse and imagine it, ponder it, meditate on it, ask the Holy Spirit to make it come alive to you. There are many verses like this. Psalm 84: what a wonderful word picture for us to imagine.

> *"How amiable are thy tabernacles, O Lord of hosts![1] My soul longeth, yea, even fainteth for the courts of the Lord: my heart and my flesh crieth out for the living God.[2] For a day in thy courts is better than a thousand. I had rather be a doorkeeper in the house of my God, than to dwell in the tents of wickedness."*[10]

Psalm 84:1,10

And a few others: Psalm 93:1, Psalm 104:1-3. I do imagine going to His throne, kneeling at His feet. I even go further, and picture him taking my hand, smiling and drawing me into his big, strong fatherly arms, holding me like a loving father would. He comforts me, causing every fear and hurt to dispel, bringing security that I've never known before. I feel deeply loved, nurtured and accepted; being held by the one who created the stars. After all, it was for us they were created, to dream under, and to see the vision that God has called us to. He is so powerful; I can picture the mere movement of His finger that causes lightning and thunder. In Revelation 21:3 it speaks of God living with us, dwelling with us. Oh, the day when we will see Him face to face!

He Uses People

Another way He loves us is through other people. Our compassion and love for one another comes from God. Think back in your own life. For me, there have been times when I felt down and needed encouragement. Then the phone would ring with an invitation to dinner! Later in the evening, for example, I would receive a warm hug from a friend at church. Fellowship comes from God, and He knows when we need comfort. The body of Christ ministers to one another.

God Can Touch Us Through Others

A few years ago, I was working at a hospital in the Admitting Department, registering patients. Having just made the decision to come to Colorado Springs to attend Bible

College, I told God that I would give up everything for Him. That day, I went to work. As I started registering a woman who was getting cancer treatment (her husband accompanied her as usual), we had a chance to visit while doing paper-work. I found out that they were also Christians, and told them of my plans to go to Bible College. When we said our goodbyes, the husband hugged me just like a loving father. I didn't know him, but somehow, in that special moment, I felt the Father's love as if to say, "I'm proud of you."

Here is another true story of God's caring nature through some close friends of mine, Herb and Linda. Herb worked at a nearby mini-market in our neighborhood, and while he was watching the news he noticed the picture of a young teen boy who lived nearby. He was missing. When Herb went to work that evening he noticed a Xeroxed picture of the boy, and brought it home.

His wife Linda saw it and showed it to their daughter. She said, "Mom, we need to pray for him." Herb went back to work and who but stumbled through the door? The young boy! He walked

Relationship? But I Can't See Him...

up to the counter, disheveled and shaken and said, "I'm lost; some guys beat me up."

Herb told him to wait right there and proceeded to call the boy's dad. Our God is so good! Not only were my friend's prayers answered, but God used them to actually be part of the process of this boy's safe return home. God does miracles like this everyday, big and small, but it all comes from Him.

I remember going through a season when I missed having flowers. At my previous home I had a garden with vegetables, herbs, and different varieties of flowers. I loved to arrange my cut flowers in the house. When we moved from that house, the Lord knew my heart, and how I missed digging in the earth and planting seeds. Being outdoors was almost more important than being indoors. The buzz of the bees and the sunshine, the fresh air…oh, how I love that. Somehow, I always feel God's presence and hear his voice clearer when I am outdoors. God can share so much wisdom and comparisons about life while you are in nature. One day, I was especially missing this interaction. While I was at work, going about my business, a co-worker happened to bring me some cut roses in a vase. I almost cried while I thanked her. Later on it hit me, "These were from you Lord, weren't they?"

The next day after work I was enjoying my walk through the parking lot. It is a nice area through tall, beautiful old trees and manicured lawns. As I started up the sidewalk, right alongside of me was a beautiful daisy looking as if it was freshly cut, just for me. It is times like these, that I see how God is romancing me with His tender love, letting me know He is there and that He hasn't forgotten me. If you are not carefully watching, you could miss these small miracles of His love. It may be a gorgeous sunset or an unexpected gift from someone, but always in the end, receive it from the Lord's tender hand. It can come in the form of hugs, gifts, words of encouragement, or a friend's invitation to share lunch. There are even times when He will bring to your remembrance a favorite worship song while you are sleeping. You'll wake up with that song playing in your head. This is a special gift to you.

Every Good Thing Comes From the Father

"Every good gift and every perfect gift is from above, and cometh down from the Father of lights, with whom is no variableness, neither shadow of turning."

James 1:17

He knows your likes and dislikes; He knows every detail about you. Why wouldn't He bring someone to love you?

Regular worship helps to build your relationship with your Father. It also helps you to keep the right perspective in life. Worship puts you in the right mindset to hear God. It causes you to get your mind off of you, your problems, and the world's negativity, so that you are better able to listen and hear His voice more clearly.

"Thou wilt keep him in perfect peace, whose mind is stayed on thee: because he trusteth in thee."

Isaiah 26:3

In times of worshiping in His presence, whether it's alone or with a body of believers, I notice all the wonderful attributes of God's character. What is it like to be in God's presence? It is the most satisfying place to be. My faith is strengthened; in fact, all of the fruits of the Spirit are evident. You can sense His love that is so powerful, and a child-like joy will come over you that brings you laughter. A peace will fill the room that words cannot describe. You only perceive that all is well because there is no need to fear anything, anyone, anywhere, when you draw on the presence of God that is already inside of you.

When you close the door to the world and enter into worship, you are entering into God's world. You can't hear His voice when you stay in your worries and problems. You won't find God there. It's like the eagle that flies high, in the clear blue sky where the clean, fresh air is. He doesn't fly where the seagulls are around the trash, looking for just what they might find. It's like God is saying, "Come up higher, Child, where I am."

We, God's children, were made to live higher; to live in God's LOVE, not in worry and fear; in strife, gossip, and jealousy. Come up where God is, live by faith and allow Him to carry your cares. When you are down in the dumps, worship your Heavenly Father, even if you don't feel like it. Worshiping is an act of your will. A decision. Lift up your hands and thank Him for His promises and the good things in your life. Allow him to move in you. However you communicate with Him, through worshipful dance or fervent prayer, allow Him to connect with you, and He will soon lift you out of your doldrums. When you give God quality time, He gives back to you in abundance!

Before too long, the Spirit's feeling inside of you is so strong that it is God Who is magnified, not your problems. The Fruits of the Spirit are evident and because of His presence, you feel love, peace and joy. Hopefulness replaces hopelessness. Worship also puts things into the right perspective. There is so much more to life, and God desires to bring a fullness and completeness that cannot be experienced without Him.

"For I know the thoughts that I think toward you, saith the Lord, thoughts of peace, and not of evil, to give you an expected end.[11] *Then shall ye call upon me, and ye shall go and pray unto me, and I will hearken unto*

you.[12] And ye shall seek me, and find me, when ye shall search for me with all your heart.[13] And I will be found of you, saith the Lord."[14]

Jeremiah 29:11-14

The Importance of His Word

The surest way to know God is through His word. By searching the Scriptures and meditating on His Word, and even by praying in tongues, you will come to know the Father and His character. The Holy Spirit will open and unravel the Scriptures to you as you take the time and make the time to meditate. Find out about His character and what He is like. Most people don't care to make the effort, but I promise you, if you are determined, you will have the time of your life. For God is full of adventure and His Word is alive and powerful. The world thinks that the Bible is absolutely boring. What they don't know is that there are hidden treasures in this powerful Book. It is a quest that will always satisfy, and will never end nor be limited. As we wrap up this chapter, here are some Scriptures you can meditate and study on:

God is Love (1 John 4:8).

Love never fails (1 Corinthians 13:8).

Love is patient, Love is kind (1 Corinthians 13:4-8).

"But this shall be the covenant that I will make with the house of Israel; After those days, saith the Lord, I will put my law in their inward parts, and write it in their hearts; and will be their God, and they shall be my people.[33] And they shall teach no more every man his neighbour, and every man his brother, saying, Know the Lord: for they shall all know me, from the least of them unto the greatest of them, saith the Lord: for I will forgive their iniquity, and I will remember their sin no more."[34]

Jeremiah 31:33-34

"And God saw every thing that he had made, and, behold, it was very good."

Genesis 1:31

"And call no man your father upon the earth: for one is your Father, which is in heaven."

Matthew 23:9

Chapter 7

OUR AIM IS TO KNOW GOD

It is a wise father that knows his own child.

-William Shakespeare

God the Father desires for you to not only know His word, but to have a personal relationship with Him, as well. Read this chapter slowly and take it all in, my friend, because this chapter could change your life. To know God is truly the aim of the Christian life. To know God your Father is what life is really all about. Without His relationship, you merely exist; but with His sweet, intimate friendship, you can live an abundant life!

God Delights in Loving You

"Thus saith the Lord, Let not the wise man glory in his wisdom, neither let the mighty man glory in his might, let not the rich man glory in his

*riches:*²³ *But let him that glorieth glory in this, that he understandeth and knoweth me, that I am the Lord which exercise lovingkindness, judgment, and righteousness, in the earth: for in these things I delight, saith the Lord."*²⁴

Jeremiah 9:23-24

Verse 24 in the Amplified says:

"But let him who glories glory in this: that he understands and knows Me [personally and practically, directly discerning and recognizing My character]."

According to Strong's, "to know" is the Hebrew word "Yada." It means, "an intimate knowing or friendship." It is the way God knows us in Psalm 139:2, "When we sit and when we rise, when we go out or come in." It is the way He knew Moses "face to face" (Exodus 37:17), and the way Adam knew Eve (Genesis 4:1). God knows every detail of our lives. Our thoughts. Our dreams.

But Jeremiah 9:23-24 explains that God wants us also to know Him this way: to know that He is a God that acts in loving kindness. This gives Him pleasure. Most people cannot understand what this means. For some, this takes a great stretch of imagination. Unbelievers cannot understand such a thing. Even believers often forget to go to the Father on a personal and intimate level, becoming consumed with making their faith work for wealth or healing. Sometimes we forget the true purpose of life: to know Him. God wants you to spend time and enjoy Him as your Heavenly Father, just for the sake of being with Him; not asking for anything, just loving Him and being with Him.

Dates With God

The one that I love to be with most is God. To have "Him and I" time is a joy. Sometimes I tell God, "Ok God, it's time for our date night." Spending time in worship is not only refreshing to me, but it pleases Him. These are my richest times: meditating on His word and intimately praying with Him. Making His Word come alive! What God has offered to us is a personal, intimate relationship… we can KNOW HIM! What an honor. What a privilege. To know the Living God with the knowledge that this is what He has intended for us from the very beginning. Hallelujiah! Glory to God!

Enjoy God's Company

God is not boring; He has an amazing sense of humor, and is a wonderful companion. He is so full of wisdom and creativity. God wants to be the "love" of our lives! There will be times when I put on upbeat praise music, and just dance. Other times I have experienced wonderful, memorable times working in my garden. While I go about my weeding, I talk to Him and listen while He reveals spiritual parallels, comparing the plants and flowers, bringing Scriptures to my remembrance. Remember that His Spirit lives in you, and is only a breath away.

Growing all varieties of seeds has run in my family for generations, as well as the pure joy and love of watching each herb, flower or vegetable come to fruition! Grandma used to plant anything and everything in whatever container that she could find. Tiny growing seedlings were found everywhere in her home. Those who love to garden understand the simple joy in a tiny flower blossom or herb. This all comes from God. We are made in His image, and I can imagine our Father receiving untelling joy and gratification as He watches His children flourish in His creation

When you walk away from reading your Bible or your daily devotion, you don't leave Him there. He always goes with you (Acts 17:27-28)! If He is always with you, then He can hear you and you should be able to hear Him. I believe that takes some practice. We must practice His presence. Practice sensing Him there with you. We think that because we don't see Him, He isn't there, and so we must lean on His Word that says, He will never leave us or forsake us (Hebrews 13:5).

How would it be if you were married, but never spoke with your wife or husband? How could a relationship grow in that setting? It cannot. It would deteriorate after time. We must nurture our physical relationships and our spiritual relationship with God, as well. I have found Him even in trivial tasks, like washing dishes! It sounds so silly, but I've grown to like washing dishes because of that.

Especially for me, His creativity is so evident in all of the spices and herbs He has made for us to enjoy. Next time you take a whiff of basil and say, "Ahhhhh," remember that the herbs and spices we enjoy are evidence of His creativity!

You see, now, how just one hour of reading His Word and then going your way doesn't cut it? You must include Him in every aspect of your life. Since He is with you wherever you go, why not acknowledge Him? Remember, the more of His Word you know, the more you will be able to discern His voice. John 14:23 says, "If a man love me, he will keep My words; and My Father will love him, and We will come unto him, and make our abode with him." Much of what we experience in God's presence is the Holy Spirit (John 14:26). They are One. They each have Their own personality. You will begin, as time goes on, to know the voice of each One. Don't struggle with it. Be patient with yourself and enjoy it as you learn.

> *"For I know the thoughts and plans that I have for you, says the Lord, thoughts and plans for welfare and peace and not for evil, to give you hope in your final outcome.[11] Then you will call upon Me, and you will come and pray to Me, and I will hear and heed you.[12] Then you will seek Me, inquire for, and require Me [as a vital necessity] and*

find Me when you search for Me with all your heart.[13] *I will be found by you, says the Lord..."*[14a]

Jeremiah 29:11-14a (Amplified)

He longs to be a vital necessity in our lives, where we can't live without Him each day. The best part of it is that you can be "yourself" in front of Him. You can fall on your face and cry out before Him. You can be totally honest with Him.

By nature, I am a very private person; basically, reserved. But not in in front of the Lord! He knows all about me, so what in the world is there for me to hide? Go ahead and be yourself in front of Him. We think that when we are saved, eternal life is just "our place in heaven." Yes, that is true, but Scripture promises us so much more!

> *"And this is eternal life: [it means] to know (to perceive, recognize, become acquainted with, and understand) You, the only true and real God, and [likewise] to know Him, Jesus [as the] Christ (the Anointed One, the Messiah), Whom You have sent."*

John 17:3 (Amplified)

Real life, exciting, abundant life begins when we know Him, the living God, the only true and real God.

Only One Can Satisfy

There is a longing in our hearts that can only be filled by knowing and receiving God's deep love for us. No other love will restore and complete you as His love can. Man is limited, but your God has absolutely no limits. Only He knows you inside and out; past, present, and future. Only He is able to meet all your needs and protect you like none other. Only God your Father has a plan for your life that is good, and only He is capable of getting you there by directing your steps. Only God gave His only Son for you, to die for you, and provide you with eternal life with Him. Only God has the power to forgive all of your sins. Only God could fill you with His own life and power; to enable you to live an abundant, victorious life on this side of heaven. For all eternity. God alone made the amazing sunrises for you to wake up to, and the millions of stars at night to dream by and imagine His mysteries! God made the powerful ocean waves that refresh your soul, demonstrating His power and might. There is a multitude of great and majestic wonders that only He has created for you out of love. Who can name them all? He is so great! Praise God, our Father Jehovah!

> "For the Father himself loveth you, because ye have loved me, and have believed that I came out from God."
>
> *John 16:27*

> "The person who has My commands and keeps them is the one who [really] loves Me; and whoever [really] loves Me will be loved by My Father, and I [too] will love him and will show (reveal, manifest) Myself to him. [I will let Myself be clearly seen by him and make Myself real to him.]"
>
> *John 14:21, AMP*

Life Is In The Present

To seek first the kingdom of God and His righteousness; to put God first in your life, you must learn to enjoy Him right now. Don't be distracted by all of your wants and needs, by your past or by your future. Too many people want change and their future immediately. Remember life is in the "now." It's not in the past. That is already gone. And it's not in the future; that's not here yet.

Think of the seasons. In the summer, you can't make winter come. No matter how bad you want it to snow; if it's summertime, it's summer. You will miss the enjoyment of summer if you're fretting for the winter to come. It's like the person who loves fall and the changing colors of the leaves. They are dreaming of pumpkins and soup making; longing for cooler air to come.

With each season, though, is something special because God made it, and all that He made is good. While you are longing for fall, you are missing out on the outdoor barbecues and drinking sweet tea with your friends. You will never have this sunset; for tomorrow is a new day with new mercies and a completely different set of clouds displaying a new array of textures. Enjoy the now. Enjoy each breath. It is a gift. People are racing these days. Racing to accomplish their most coveted goals: that big, perfect house, the job promotion—so well-deserved. But what about TIME? I just may have to reserve that subject for another book. Perhaps. Each moment we live in is exactly where it needs to be. In the "now." In the book of Ecclesiastes it states, "To everything there is a season."

Right now is the season of "Life." There is a very valuable lesson here, if we can learn this truth.

The Father Loves

Chapter 8

THE FATHER WANTS YOU TO TRUST HIM

I cannot think of any need in childhood as strong as the need for a father's protection.

-Sigmund Freud

The Father loves it when you trust Him. Think of it: why do you think that is important? We receive everything from God through faith. Trust is another definition of faith. All the finished work that Christ has purchased for us can only be partaken of and enjoyed by faith. You can't even receive salvation without trust.

Trust: 1. Firm belief in the honesty, reliability of another; faith 2. Confident expectation, hope (Webster's Dictionary).

Trusting in Ourselves

A simple story to help us consider what trust is like:

One day, little Steven noticed that he had a broken skate-board wheel. He explains his dire need to his dad, who says, "No problem, Stevie, I'll take care of it in the morning when the sporting goods store is open."

Things should be settled, right? Wrong. Unwilling to wait, Steven begins to make his own plans. Climbing up into the kitchen cupboards, he starts making a racket of stirring and mixing. A short time later, Steven has everything under control. His dad looks out the window, puzzled to see a scribbly sign that reads LEMONADE 25 cents, and says to himself, 'Now, what's going on?'

Later on, little Stevie comes in excitedly waving three dollars. "Dad, I really didn't want to wait until tomorrow morning and, to be honest, I was worried that you might forget about me. Besides, dad, I know how busy you are," Steven explains.

Feeling disappointed in Steven's lack of faith, his dad tells him that the wheel he needs actually costs eight dollars. "Besides that, Stevie, it's Sunday and the store isn't open."

"Gee, all that hard work, and it didn't do me any good at all," Steven says under his breath. God has gone through the heights and depths and even lengths to secure our past, present and future, and we all too often try to go and sell lemonade to take care of it ourselves. Come on. How many times have I made lemonade? Only the Lord knows…and I'm not talking about the saying, "When life gives you lemons, make lemonade." In other words, "God's too slow, and I'm taking things into my own hands." With all of my "lemonade money," I could have a good amount in savings right now. But, we are so limited on our own.

We Can Trust Him Completely

Psalm 37 is a wonderful Psalm about trusting in God. Here are several verses:

"Trust in the Lord, and do good; so shalt thou dwell in the land, and verily thou shalt be fed.[3] *Delight thyself also in*

the Lord: and he shall give thee the desires of thine heart.[4] *Commit thy way unto the Lord; trust also in him; and he shall bring it to pass.*[5] *And he shall bring forth thy righteousness as the light, and thy judgment as the noonday.*[6] *Rest in the Lord, and wait patiently for him…*[7] *The steps of a good man are ordered by the Lord: and he delighteth in his way..*[23] *Though he fall, he shall not be utterly cast down: for the Lord upholdeth him with his hand.*[24] *I have been young, and now am old; yet have I not seen the righteous forsaken, nor his seed begging bread."*[25] *The law of his God is in his heart; none of his steps shall slide.*[31] *Wait on the Lord, and keep his way, and he shall exalt thee to inherit the land: when the wicked are cut off, thou shalt see it."*[34]

Psalm 37:3-7,23-25,31,34

It's wonderful, the whole Psalm. Read it all, and it ends with Trust!

"And the Lord shall help them, and deliver them: he shall deliver them from the wicked, and save them, because they trust in him."[40]

Psalm 37:40

Some would think it reckless to trust in a being they cannot see. But it is with reckless abandon that we **can** trust Him, as if going out on a limb. God always proves Himself faithful. Look back on your past experiences when you know that He has provided. You know which ones I'm talking about. Remember the "awe" which strengthened you to trust in Him again?

If you notice in the Psalm, there are three "trusts." The first two are different from the very last. The first two "trusts" in the Hebrew are "Batah," shown 103 times in the Bible, which means, "to trust, be confident, sure, and be bold, to have hope" (#982 Strong's).

The last Hebrew word for trust is "Kasa" and is found 35 times in the Bible, and it means, "to flee for protection, make refuge, confide in" (#2620 Strong's). God is faithful, and loves when his children trust him. Here are some more verses on trust:

"But he that trusteth in the Lord, mercy shall compass him about."

Psalm 32:10

"The Lord is good, a strong hold in the day of trouble; and he knoweth them that trust in him."

Nahum 1:7

"The Lord redeemeth the soul of his servants: and none of them that trust in him shall be desolate."

Psalm 34:22

"And they that know thy name will put their trust in thee: for thou, Lord, hast not forsaken them that seek thee."

Psalm 9:10

"The Lord is my strength and my shield; my heart trusted in him, and I am helped: therefore my heart greatly rejoiceth; and with my song will I praise him."

Psalm 28:7

The Father Wants You to Trust Him

"O taste and see that the Lord is good: blessed is the man that trusteth in him.[8] O fear the Lord, ye his saints: for there is no want to them that fear him.[9] The young lions do lack, and suffer hunger: but they that seek the Lord shall not want any good thing."[10]

Psalm 34:8-10

"But I am like a green olive tree in the house of God: I trust in the mercy of God for ever and ever."

Psalm 52:8

"What time I am afraid, I will trust in thee.[3] In God I will praise his word, in God I have put my trust; I will not fear what flesh can do unto me."[4]

Psalm 56:3-4

"Trust in him at all times; ye people, pour out your heart before him: God is a refuge for us."

Psalm 62:8

"But it is good for me to draw near to God: I have put my trust in the Lord God, that I may declare all thy works."

Psalm 73:28

"He shall not be afraid of evil tidings: his heart is fixed, trusting in the Lord."

Psalm 112:7

"Trust in the Lord with all thine heart; and lean not unto thine own understanding.⁵ In all thy ways acknowledge him, and he shall direct thy paths."⁶

Proverbs 3:5-6

"Every word of God is pure: he is a shield unto them that put their trust in him."

Proverbs 30:5

"Blessed is the man that trusteth in the Lord, and whose hope the Lord is.⁷ For he shall be as a tree planted by the waters, and that spreadeth out her roots by the river, and shall not see when heat cometh, but her leaf shall be green;

and shall not be careful in the year of drought, neither shall cease from yielding fruit."[8]

Jeremiah 17:7-8

"Who delivered us from so great a death, and doth deliver: in whom we trust that he will yet deliver us."

2 Corinthians 1:10

"For God so loved the world, that he gave his only begotten Son, that whosoever believeth in him should not perish, but have everlasting life."

John 3:16

The word "believeth" here is the Greek word "pisteuo," which means, "to have faith, entrust, and commit to" (Strong's #4100).

"For God so greatly loved and dearly prized the world that He [even] gave up His only begotten (unique) Son, so that whoever believes in (trusts in, clings to, relies on)

Him shall not perish (come to destruction, be lost) but have eternal (everlasting) life."

John 3:16 (Amplified)

"This is how much God loved the world: He gave his Son, his one and only Son. And this is why: so that no one need be destroyed; by believing in him, anyone can have a whole and lasting life. God didn't go to all the trouble of sending his Son merely to point an accusing finger, telling the world how bad it was. He came to help, to put the world right again. Anyone who trusts in him is acquitted; anyone who refuses to trust him has long since been under the death sentence without knowing it. And why? Because of that person's failure to believe in the one-of-a-kind Son of God when introduced to him."

John 3:16 (Message)

I strongly encourage you to take these Scriptures one at a time, jot them down on a card, and meditate on them throughout the day. This is what I did. It is the reason you are reading this book, "The Father Loves," right now. I never would have gone to Bible college or dreamed and believed for the things I do now. As I began to meditate, more and more of God's Word began to come alive in me. I was able to understand its great value. Take advantage of the Scriptures included in the pages of this book; if even one of the verses speak to you, memorize it or write it down. My home is filled with verses that are very special to me, which I have written (and typed) for encouragement, and to just simply feel His presence.

If you put these good seeds in your heart, they can spring to life and grow. The Word of God will change your life if you let it. Praise God forever! Praise the Lord Jehovah! He is worthy to be praised! We can trust Him because He is faithful forever! He loves us. It is truly up to you to do this. No one can do this for you. It is possible to be saved and never partake of the promises Jesus has paid for. Or you can enjoy them on this side of heaven. God did not mean for us to just "hang on" until heaven comes.

God Prizes You

Think of your own children; how greatly you prize and protect them. With great love you care for them; you think of them and what is best for them constantly. Remember when your children were young and you took them on an outing—maybe a city your family had never gone to before? Remember the extra care you took in watching over them. And then, when they were teenagers, you watched them even closer... with the eyes of a hawk! How *much more* does God care for you? The love of God watches over you so much more!

A Wake Up Call to Trust Him

In 2008, many people in California suffered from foreclosure; I was one of them. This was approximately the same time that I was praying about going to Bible School in Colorado. Sometimes it takes time to learn the valuable lesson of trust; you continue learning it as you grow older. To transplant My life to a completely different state is something I've never experienced before, but the desire to go wouldn't leave, and I had to make a

The Father Wants You to Trust Him

decision. One day I sat down with the Lord and told Him of all my concerns with moving and taking this huge leap of faith. I told Him, as if He didn't know, "Lord, I'm not in my 20's anymore…I'm a single woman now… It would be crazy to uproot my whole life."

I kept telling Him each one of my worries, with my son who lived with me at the time being my biggest concern. In my heart, I heard the Lord say, "If I took care of your son and of all the things you are concerned about, then would you go?" I thought about it for just a moment and said, "Yes, yes of course I would."

He said, "Consider them done." And He was true to His word. One by one, they were taken care of. Yes, I prayed for the miracle that my house wouldn't foreclose, but at the same time, I was losing the desire to stay and keep it. I started to have peace in my heart to let it go completely. Colossians 3:15 speaks of how we are to let God's peace rule in our hearts regarding everything. My heart was to follow the Lord's plan for my life, so little by little He helped me by giving me wisdom.

God put it on My friends' hearts to help pack and move Me. Good grief, there was so much stuff! I gave my washer and dryer away, the fridge, and a lot of furniture. It met the needs of others, and I was learning to trust my Lord. Someone offered to pull a trailer and move Me across the states. My Son also came with us and helped, and God took care of Him just as He promised. He did a series of miracles to get me to Colorado, and it wasn't easy leaving My family, but living by faith requires risk, and God was teaching Me just that.

While I was first getting settled in Colorado Springs, I started making a lot of decisions on My own with very limited success. Debt was starting to accumulate; I was running out of funds, and the rent was soon due. By this time, school had started, and seven months went by with me living there; I needed to learn more on the lesson of trust. Sometimes it takes us awhile to learn life's lessons. I asked God, "What's going on? What am I doing wrong?"

One day I finally listened, and I heard God ask, "Who is your Lord?" I answered, "You are." He said "Oh, really?" The verse came to me from Psalm 23:1, "The Lord is my Shepherd, I shall not want." I saw that I wasn't giving Him all of me, such as my finances, my decisions, my time, and all of my trust. He still only

The Father Wants You to Trust Him

had part of me. I loved His Word dearly, and had moved across states, left my job, family and my world back in California. Yet, I still kept control of certain things.

I remember this day so vividly:

I sat on the living room carpet on my knees, praying, "Lord, I am alone and in a strange new place. I've been carrying a heavy load and feeling like I am responsible for taking care of everything myself. Forgive me, Father. I give You all of me, and I acknowledge You as My Shepherd. I know that You will care for me much better than I have; I don't know what's ahead, but I know you only mean good for my life." After throwing my hands in the air, I gave Him my life, my hopes and my future. I can even remember how free that I felt; light as a feather!

I was holding the reins in my life, but only getting problems, limitations, and absolutely NO fruit. God showed Me that He was the One who needed to hold the reins of my life, and if I gave them over to Him, in absolute trust, I would not only have peace, but NO limits and plenty of fruit. It is possible to give God some of the areas in your life, yet keep ahold of others. Having a shepherd means you must learn to follow. He gives us a free will so we can follow willingly. A shepherd protects, cares, provides, feeds, defends, and leads. When someone else leads, it takes the pressure off you. Remember that your Creator knows best. He has a plan for your life, but it's His plan. How stuck are you on your plan? Have you done any better? Do you think you could do better? Can you see ahead into your future? God can, and He will reveal things to you at the right times, but only if you let Him.

Since I have allowed God to lead me in all areas of my life, He has led me to wonderful avenues, provided for all of my needs, blessed me in ways I wouldn't have asked for, and opened up surprising doors of opportunity. Being with God is an adventure! Trusting in Him is so much better than trusting in myself or, for that matter, anyone else. As long as we are here on this earth, we will always be learning more and more about trusting God. He will never steer you wrong. He only has blessings in store for you, my friend; only good things, only perfect things.

Chapter 9

LET GOD SPEAK

All I have seen teaches me to trust the Creator for all I have not seen.

-Ralph Waldo Emerson

"My sheep hear my voice, and I know them, and they follow me."

John 10:27

"For I know the thoughts that I think toward you, saith the Lord, thoughts of peace, and not of evil, to give you an expected end.[11] *Then shall ye call upon me, and ye shall go and pray unto me, and I will hearken unto you.*[12] *And ye shall seek me, and find*

> *me, when ye shall search for me with all your heart.*[13] *And I will be found of you, saith the Lord."*[14]

> **Jeremiah 29:11-14**

God speaks through His Word, and if you're saved, He is in you and will never leave you. He goes where we go, sees what we see and hears what we hear, and even hears what we say and knows what we think. Our Father knows what is on our minds and hearts.

Why can't He talk to us, then, and why shouldn't we be able to hear Him? Once again:

> *"He knows the secrets of the heart."*

> **Psalm 44:21, AMP**

He called us friends, and friends have fellowship. A true friend listens to you, cries with you, laughs with you, and is one whom you can confide in. Remember that "Koinonia"" is the Greek word for fellowship. Fellowship is both partaking, both talking and both listening.

"But I have called you friends; for all things that I have heard of my Father I have made known unto you.⁵ Ye have not chosen me, but I have chosen you."¹⁶

John 15:15-16

He Prizes Your Uniqueness

Did you know that God is interested in you, and is living through your very own personality uniquely? He made only one you. He wants to show Himself strong through you; not to ignore or forget about you. You are a co-laborer with God. He is not a robot, nor does He want robots for kids. He's a father and knows that each child in His family is completely different; with personal likes and dislikes. That's okay with Him, and in fact, He encourages it, and loves for you to be unique and creative. Otherwise, why would He have created so many different, unique animals?

Think of it: a tall, skinny–legged, golden spotted giraffe with a long tongue; a pink-as-pink-can-be flamingo that stands on one twiggy leg. A huge black whale that spouts water and sings under the deep blue ocean. God definitely has a sense of humor! Did you know that there are 28,000 different types of butterflies in this world, with most species found in the tropics? Think of all the millions of species of flowers, not to mention their colors. Think of all the wonderful trees! A variety of colors, textures, and sounds; God created everything uniquely…just like you!

You may have read in Philippians 1:21, "For to me to live is Christ, and to die is gain." Or in John 3:30, "He must increase, but I must decrease." I know we have to read the entirety of these chapters to understand what their exact meaning is, but I used to think that God didn't exactly want me, myself, or my personality—but only Jesus living through me. I would read these Scriptures and strive for this as my goal. But quite frankly, I misunderstood these Scriptures to say that I didn't matter. I was wrong.

What they are referring to is our will—what we want to accomplish in life and our own agenda—should be secondary to God's plans and purposes. We should be focusing on what He wants to accomplish through us, our personality and our own unique characteristics. The reason is because He has a better and more perfect plan for our lives than our own. His plans will make us happier and bless others. God loves your uniqueness and your personality; He doesn't want to get rid of that. He wants to share your life with you, and have new adventures together.

Why did God create different colors of people and different types of voices? Some sing alto, some soprano, and some sing with a deep bass voice. If God wanted to cross you out and only let Himself speak and act through a body, He could have made us all look and sound the same. He could have made every tree the same. He might even have made only one type of flower throughout the whole entire world. Wow, what would that look like? Only yellow daisies everywhere; only pine trees everywhere. What if the only animal was a penguin? What if everyone spoke the same, ate the same thing, and drove the same car?

I believe we can safely say and agree that God is a God who loves variety, and that He has a special plan for all of us. He enjoys our uniquenesses, our gifts, talents and abilities, and we can choose to what extent we will live out the plans and purposes He has for our lives.

Many Facets to a Friendship

Why do we think that God will only fellowship with us if we're doing something holy? Do you think He is only interested in you when you go to church or read your Bible? Do you picture His voice sounding like the old fashion King James Bible version, only speaking in "thees and thous?" Listen, now. This is important in hearing His voice. He will speak through *your* thoughts, *your* vocabulary, and *your* personality on a level that *you* can understand. Sometimes, you may have heard Him, but could have dismissed His voice, assuming that you were hearing your own thoughts. I used to think that God was only interested in speaking to me about the Scriptures, but He has enlightened me using my music and many other interests of mine. After all, God is the master of every song note, every color and every design! It's not too difficult to perceive that His interest in our lives exceeds what we could ever possibly imagine!

"Every good gift and every perfect gift is from above, and cometh down from the Father of lights, with whom is no variableness, neither shadow of turning."

James 1:17

He Has Come to Stay

"Jesus answered and said unto him, If a man love me, he will keep my words: and my Father will love him, and we will come unto him, and make our abode with him."

John 14:23

Abode/ Meno: A staying residence; to abide, to continue.

If God lives in you, then He's always there, no matter what you're involved in. You are His prized creation, and He wants to be a part of your everyday life. Allow Him to come and help you. Your life can bring God so much glory just by acknowledging His presence; asking for His touch and guidance in everything you do. Don't ever think that what you are doing isn't important. He loves to see you excel at whatever you put your hands to.

The Father Loves

In the end, remember to acknowledge and thank Him for the wonderful results!

> *"Hear, O my people, and I will testify unto thee: O Israel, if thou wilt hearken unto me;[8] There shall no strange god be in thee; neither shalt thou worship any strange god.[9] I am the Lord thy God, which brought thee out of the land of Egypt: open thy mouth wide, and I will fill it.[10] But my people would not hearken to my voice; and Israel would none of me.[11] So I gave them up unto their own hearts' lust: and they walked in their own counsels.[12] Oh that my people had hearkened unto me, and Israel had walked in my ways![13] I should soon have subdued their enemies, and turned my hand against their adversaries.[14] The haters of the Lord should have submitted themselves unto him: but their time should have endured for ever.[15] He should have fed them also with the finest of the wheat: and with honey out of the rock should I have satisfied thee."[16]*

> ***Psalm 81:8-16***

"Be still, and know that I am God."

Psalm 46:10

"Call unto me, and I will answer thee, and show thee great and mighty things, which thou knowest not."

Jeremiah 33:3

"For we are made partakers of Christ, if we hold the beginning of our confidence stedfast unto the end;[14] While it is said, To day if ye will hear his voice, harden not your hearts, as in the provocation.[15] For some, when they had heard, did provoke: howbeit not all that came out of Egypt by Moses."[16]

Hebrews 3:14-16

Before Jesus died on the cross, He prayed to God His Father about the disciples and all of us who would come. Do you know what one of His heart's desires was? Read John chapter 17 to hear some of His prayer. Here are some of the last words of Jesus to His disciples:

"And this is life eternal, that they might know thee the only true God, and Jesus Christ, whom thou hast sent.³ That they all may be one; as thou, Father, art in me, and I in thee, that they also may be one in us: that the world may believe that thou hast sent me.²¹ And the glory which thou gavest me I have given them; that they may be one, even as we are one:²² I in them, and thou in me, that they may be made perfect in one; and that the world may know that thou hast sent me, and hast loved them, as thou hast loved me.²³ And I have declared unto them thy name, and will declare it: that the love wherewith thou hast loved me may be in them, and I in them."²⁶

John 17:3,21-23,26

The whole chapter is glorious. If you were to die, what would some of your last words be? Isn't it amazing to think that He was thinking and praying for us with such compassion and tender thoughts of love?

Remember that we can hear the Holy Spirit speaking at any time and at any place, under any circumstance. Picture this: you're at Niagara Falls…deafening, thunderous water is rushing all around you. You can't even hear what the person is shouting next to you, but you can hear your Father speak within you, in that very still small voice. He might say, "Isn't this magnificent? I made it just for you because I love you."

Don't get frustrated if at first you think you can't hear His voice. He might desire to have a conversation with you, but sometimes we get too distracted. The more you read the Word of God, the more you will be able to discern His voice. He will never contradict Himself, and His words will always line up with the Bible. For example, He will never tell you to jump off a bridge because John 10:10 says, "I came that they might have life, and that they might have it more abundantly." If you don't know His Word, then you won't know if He is speaking. Sometimes, you might be wondering if it is you! It is reading the Word of God that helps you to discern His voice. Be patient with yourself, and enjoy getting to know Him through His Word.

The Father Loves

Chapter 10

GOD SINGS OVER YOU

The aim and final end of all music should be none other than the glory of God and the refreshment of the soul.

-Johann Sebastian Bach

Why do we sing, and where did this way of opening our mouths to exclaim words with notes and melodies come from?

"Let Us make man in Our image, according to Our likeness."

Genesis 1:26 (NKJV)

Singing Comes From God

He's the One Who made us this way. The birds twitter and melodiously whistle. Bees hum. Whales sing. Dogs howl.

Toddlers sing when they're just playing. No one teaches them; He made them that way.

Sing: 1. To produce musical sounds with the voice 2. To use song or verse in praise 3. To make musical sounds as a songbird (Webster's New World Dictionary).

Singing helps our hearts express what words cannot. It's as if we're so full, we can't help it. It must come out in song. Singing expresses our emotions. When we're happy and in love, we sing. When we are sad and forlorn, singing may be a form of lamentation. We see in Genesis that we were made in God's image. Then, surely, God must sing.

One of my favorite singers is Andrea Bocelli. Wow, what a voice. Some friends of mine went to see him in concert…I can just imagine it. When someone sings like that and you are in the same room, you are instantly raptured into another realm of such joy and deep emotion. I can remember being a music major in college, and during one of our recitals, there was a young man who was a bit stout, with very plain features. When it was his turn to sing, he chose an Aria from an Italian opera. His voice had such a warm tone, so powerful and moving that it sent chills up and down your spine. Everyone in the room stopped, and was spellbound.

Singing is very powerful. If someone is singing on stage, they have the power to reach into the very depths of the soul of another human being. When listening with an open heart, they will receive exactly what is being conveyed.

The calling on my life is to sing, and I've have had the privilege of being a worship leader in churches for many years. I have seen when a person is not receiving the Word of God in preaching due to a hard heart, but oftentimes their heart will soften through the listening of praise music. That's why worship is usually first in a church service; to allow us to express our thankful hearts in praise, and to prepare our hearts to receive the message. Singing as one body to the One True God is exhilarating and wonderfully refreshing. When we get to Heaven, there will be so much joy, there will be no other way to express it, than by singing and dancing.

Let's read some of examples in the Word. Miriam led in song:

> *"And Miriam...took a timbrel in her hand; and all the women went out after her with timbrels and with dances.[20] And Miriam answered them, Sing ye to the Lord, for he hath triumphed gloriously; the horse and his rider hath he thrown into the sea."[21]*
>
> ***Exodus 15:20-21***

This was after God did one of the greatest miracles of all time, and parted the Red Sea so the children of Israel could cross on dry land. They got to the other side, and couldn't contain themselves! They sang and danced, for the victory of God was so great! They had never seen anything like it, who could do such a thing? The horse and rider thrown into the sea...read the whole chapter in Exodus 15 to see the song that Moses and the children of Israel sang. It's right to praise God when victory comes. Here's an excerpt from that song:

> *"The Lord is a man of war: the Lord is his name.[3] Pharaoh's chariots and his host hath he cast into the*

> *sea: his chosen captains also are drowned in the Red sea.⁴ The depths have covered them: they sank into the bottom as a stone.⁵ Thy right hand, O Lord, is become glorious in power: thy right hand, O Lord, hath dashed in pieces the enemy.⁶ And with the blast of thy nostrils the waters were gathered together, the floods stood upright as an heap, and the depths were congealed in the heart of the sea.⁸*
>
> ***Exodus 15:3-6,8***

We have read how the children of Israel were often up and down, one minute rejoicing in God and the next complaining. But think about how, at this particular moment, God must have been so pleased as He watched them rejoicing in His power and might! You can picture even the angels dancing and shouting!

Let's go now to a passage where David danced. Even though we're speaking of singing, dancing is similar in that there is a need to express the heart.

> *"And it was so, that when they that bare the ark of the Lord had gone six paces, he sacrificed oxen and*

fatlings.[13] *And David danced before the Lord with all his might; and David was girded with a linen ephod.*[14] *So David and all the house of Israel brought up the ark of the Lord with shouting, and with the sound of the trumpet."*[15]

2 Samuel 6:13-15

In Hebrew the word "Danced" is "Paneh," which means, "to whirl and to dance" (Strong's #3769). When you're so full of joy inside that you can't contain it, you must express it!

Lucifer, The Anointed Cherub

In order to understand that "Song" comes from God, we need to take a look at a passage where we find out how Satan, originally called Lucifer, was created. Although he is now defeated, he was created by God to serve in worship and in song.

Ezekiel 27 and 28 are speaking about the King of Tyrus. You may be wondering why Satan is linked with the city of Tyre, a famous commercial city of Phoenicia on the coast of the Mediterranean. Tyre means, "a rock." This city was rich in merchandise and trade, but became evil with greed, thus the link with Satan. They had an industry where a certain type of shellfish created a purple dye, in which they used to dye material used for royalty. Remember the Scripture in 1 Timothy 6:10, "The love of money is the root of all evil." Greed for riches will cause many to fall.

> *"Moreover the word of the Lord came unto me, saying,[11] Son of man, take up a lamentation upon the king of Tyrus, and say unto him, Thus saith the Lord God; Thou sealest up the sum, full of wisdom, and perfect in beauty.[12] Thou hast been in Eden the garden of God; every precious stone was thy covering, the sardius, topaz, and the diamond, the beryl, the onyx, and the jasper, the sapphire, the emerald, and the carbuncle, and gold: the workmanship of thy tabrets and of thy pipes was prepared in thee in the day that thou wast created.[13] Thou art the anointed cherub that covereth; and I have set thee so: thou wast upon the holy mountain of God; thou hast walked up and down in the midst of the stones of fire.[14] Thou wast perfect in thy ways from the day that thou wast created, till iniquity was found in thee.[15] By the multitude of thy*

merchandise they have filled the midst of thee with violence, and thou hast sinned: therefore I will cast thee as profane out of the mountain of God: and I will destroy thee, O covering cherub, from the midst of the stones of fire[16] *Thine heart was lifted up because of thy beauty, thou hast corrupted thy wisdom by reason of thy brightness: I will cast thee to the ground, I will lay thee before kings, that they may behold thee.*[17] *Thou hast defiled thy sanctuaries by the multitude of thine iniquities, by the iniquity of thy traffick; therefore will I bring forth a fire from the midst of thee, it shall devour thee, and I will bring thee to ashes upon the earth in the sight of all them that behold thee.*[18] *All they that know thee among the people shall be astonished at thee: thou shalt be a terror, and never shalt thou be any more.*[19]

Ezekiel 28:11-19

I wondered why God made Lucifer so beautiful. He created him with the workmanship of tabrets (tambourines and rhythm) and pipes (pipes, or some type of woodwinds, flutes) to be able to praise Him beautifully. Perhaps the reason that worship and praise are meant to be beautiful is because it's giving glory to God, the Creator of the Universe. Praise is meant to be lovely to God, but at the same time it nourishes us. Think about it. When you've been in a worship service, and are truly worshiping, aren't you tremendously refreshed and strengthened afterwards?

> *"Make a joyful noise unto God, all ye lands:[1] Sing forth the honour of his name: make his praise glorious."[2]*

> ***Psalm 66:1-2***

I understand this portion in Ezekiel 28, as such: that Lucifer was made beautiful to show glorious worship to God, to cover our awesome God with glory and praise through songs and music coming from the heart. But he began to accumulate his own praise because of his beauty and talents; he took his talents and caused others to worship him (by the iniquity of traffick/trade.) So Lucifer used his trade for his own glory; for his own purpose and his own gain. His wisdom was corrupted, the Word says. Another way to put it is that he allowed pride to rise up in him, which in turn corrupted his wisdom. Pride brought his fall.

Let Your Talents Glorify God, Not You

Our talents originated from God, not us. God made us. He gave us everything we have; our breath, our minds to create, our voices to sing, our hands to play instruments. The bottom line is they are meant for God's glory, to bring others to Him. We were not meant to gain vast amounts of wealth by showering others with our talents, and giving glory to ourselves. We were meant to shower and cover God with our talents and the praises of our hearts. We are in relationship with God. When you are in relationship with someone you love, the other bestows praises on you, and you on them. Let God praise you, not yourself. The issue with making yourself an idol of worship in music is destructive. It strengthens pride, which gives way to fall.

"He who hath builded the house hath more honour than the house."

Hebrews 3:3

In the New Testament, we see a verse where Jesus was angry:

"And said unto them, It is written, My house shall be called the house of prayer; but ye have made it a den of thieves."

Matthew 21:13

The Greek word for "Prayer" here is speaking of prayer and worship. Song was created by God, and was intended for worship. If we are going to sing one to another, it should also come from the heart and be shared in love. Ultimately, love nourishes us and brings thankfulness to God, causing us to do it all over again. Compare this with the rain. It comes from the clouds and waters the earth to yield its fruit, and then it happens all over again. In the end, it's all about love—God's Agape Love.

The Creator Sings

A prophetic passage of Jesus:

*"Sing, O daughter of Zion; shout, O Israel; be glad and rejoice with all the heart, O daughter of Jerusalem.[14] The Lord hath taken away thy judgments, he hath cast out thine enemy: the king of Israel, even the Lord, is in the midst of thee: thou shalt not see evil any more.[15] In that day it shall be said to Jerusalem, Fear thou not: and to Zion, Let not thine hands be slack.[16] The Lord thy **God** in the **midst** of thee is mighty; he will save, he will **rejoice** over thee with **joy;** he will **rest in his love,** he will joy over thee with singing."[17]*

Zephaniah 3:14-17

Now, let's break the down the words that are in bold:

*The Lord thy **God** in the **midst** of thee is mighty: He will save, he will **rejoice** over thee with **joy;** He will **rest in his love,** He will **joy** over thee with **singing.***

God: Speaking of the trinity, for the Hebrew word is "Elohim-Gods" (Strong's #430).

Midst: Hebrew word "Gereb," meaning the center (Strong's #7130).

Rejoice: To be bright and cheerful. To be glad (Strong's #7797).

Joy: To have blithesomeness and glee, to have exceeding gladness and mirth, pleasure (Strong's #8057).

Rest in his love: God is now resting in His love because His wrath has been satisfied with the ultimate sacrifice, Jesus (Rom. 5:9).

Joy: To spin around, under influence of any violent emotion, to rejoice (Strong's #1523).

Singing: To cry, creaking, shrill sound, shout with gladness, a proclamation, to rejoice and sing with triumph (Strong's #7440).

So you see, the Lord is excited to have redeemed you. Sometimes we think that because we are saved, we got in by the skin of our teeth. That He simply allowed us entrance into His kingdom. NO! He loved you so much, He couldn't wait for you to come and accept His work on your behalf. It was His sacrifice; He laid down His life just for you. Christ is your hero and your champion, and He treasures you, the prize that He has won. He dances and sings with delight over you, and shouts with triumph that you are His. You are His own, and you have been bought with a price. He saved you because of His great love!

The following is such a wonderful verse; I want you to see it in a few different translations:

> *"The Lord your God is in the midst of you, a Mighty One, a Savior [Who saves]! He will rejoice over you with joy; He will rest [in silent satisfaction] and in His love He will be silent and make no mention [of past sins, or even recall them]; He will exult over you with singing."*
>
> ***Zephaniah 3:17 (Amplified)***

God Sings Over You

"Your God is present among you, a strong Warrior there to save you. Happy to have you back, he'll calm you with his love and delight you with his songs."

Zephaniah 3:17 (Message)

"The Lord your God is with you, the Mighty Warrior who saves. He will take great delight in you; in his love he will no longer rebuke you, but will rejoice over you with singing."

Zephaniah 3:17 (NIV)

"For the Lord your God is living among you. He is a mighty savior. He will take delight in you with gladness. With his love, he will calm all your fears. He will rejoice over you with joyful songs."

Zephaniah 3:17 (NLT)

Accept your destiny and stop seeing yourself as a discard and unimportant. YOU are very important and valuable to the Father!

> *"Who for the joy that was set before him endured the cross…"*
>
> ***Hebrews 12:2***

What do you think the "joy" is that was set before Jesus? We are His bride, His body, His pearl of great price. The joy is you, my friend. The thought of His bride kept Him going, and I believe the thought of spending an eternity without you was more unbearable than the thought of going to the cross. You have His heart, and you are in His heart. It was you that kept Jesus going until the end.

Chapter 11

GOD GAVE HIS BEST GIFT

The greatest gift is a portion of thyself.

-Ralph Waldo Emerson

Think of your precious loved ones; those who are closest to you. One could even say those for whom you would give your life. They may be the ones you pray most for, spend the most time with, the people you love most deeply. When it comes to their birthday, you consider it very special. You never forget, and you want to make sure that their gift is very unique and memorable. You take the utmost care in choosing something they would enjoy. You want to please them, and you even picture the joy on their face when they open your gift. It is not drudgery at all! We can't wait for these birthday celebrations, and we so look forward to them.

We each have so many rich memories of these times, that we treasure them deep within our hearts. Be honest; it's not that way for every birthday party we go to. Yes, we are happy for them and pleased when they enjoy what we gave them, but it's not the same as those closest to us. It's like we are even more excited for our loved ones to open the gift than they are. We say, "Hurry up! Go and open your gift! I hope you like it!"

Now, think about God's gift. His way of thinking is quite different than the world. I know giving His Son has absolutely no comparison with anything we could ever give, but I'm talking about giving our best in our own world of experience, in a way we can relate. The world tends to show special treatment to some, and totally disregards others. You would call this being a respecter of persons, which God is not. God's gift cannot compare with anything we could ever give to anyone. You couldn't pay any amount for it. God is the author of giving! He loved the most, and He gave His best. He gave us His only Son, Jesus! *"God is NO respecter of persons."*

Acts 10:34, emphasis mine

He made every human being. They are His creation, and He loves them each the same; good and bad, righteous and evil. Yes, He loves them, each one the same.

"The Lord is not slack concerning his promise, as some men count slackness; but is longsuffering to usward, not willing that any should perish, but that all should come to repentance."

2 Peter 3:9

"How think ye? if a man have an hundred sheep, and one of them be gone astray, doth he not leave the ninety and nine, and goeth into the mountains, and seeketh that which is gone astray?[12] And if so be that he find it, verily I say unto you, he rejoiceth more of that sheep, than of the ninety and nine which went not astray.[13] Even so it is not the will of your Father which is in heaven, that one of these little ones should perish."[14]

Matthew 18:12-14

We have been trained by religion, tradition and the law to look at our works and deeds; to weigh each man by his works, whether good or evil, righteous or unrighteous. The better person is the one "deserving." The one who doesn't spend hours in prayer deserves nothing. We have believed this for so long, but now we must unlearn and get ahold of God's grace.

> *"For it is a good thing that the heart be established with grace."*
>
> ***Hebrews 13:9***

God loves EACH man, every man and the whole world the same; with such a deep fervent love, that He decided to give His best gift for all to be saved, Jesus Christ. The Father is the One Who sent His son. The Father is the One Who showed and proved His love for us, even while we were at our worst, even while we were yet sinners.

God Proved His Love

> *"For when we were yet without strength, in due time Christ died for the ungodly.[6] For scarcely for a righteous man will one die: yet peradventure for a good man some would even dare to die.[7] But God commendeth his love toward us, in that, while we were yet sinners, Christ died for us.[8] Much more then, being*

now justified by his blood, we shall be saved from wrath through him.⁹ For if, when we were enemies, we were reconciled to God by the death of his Son, much more, being reconciled, we shall be saved by his life."¹⁰

Romans 5:6-10

Would you go out of your way and give your best gift for a homeless person on drugs? Would you sacrifice your time, even lay down your life for them? God proved His love. Some people say, "I don't believe God loves me…my life is a mess…there is nothing but problems…I know He is punishing me…what do I have to do to get His attention and His love?" The Word does not lie. His Word is Truth; it states the proof of His love. He's already proven it. He doesn't need to do it again!

"God shows and clearly proves His own love for us by the fact that while we were still sinners, Christ (The Messiah, The Anointed One) died for us."

Romans 5:8 (Amplified)

> *"For God so loved the world, that he gave his only begotten Son, that whosoever believeth in him should not perish, but have everlasting life."*
>
> *John 3:16*

> *"For God so greatly loved and dearly prized the world that He [even] gave up His only begotten (unique) Son, so that whoever believes in (trusts in, clings to, relies on) Him shall not perish (come to destruction, be lost) but have eternal (everlasting) life."*
>
> *John 3:16 (Amplified)*

Beloved, if God has given His best, don't think that He is withholding anything from you. It is "in Christ" that He has given you everything. It pleased God the Father to place all rule and authority under Jesus, and to exalt the name of Jesus above all else. Full completeness has been placed in Him, and if you are one of His own, then that same completeness is in you. What a gift this is from the Father. He wants us to be complete; lacking nothing.

Filled to the Brim

This is a silly analogy in comparison, but one you may understand—one that might hit home. If you will remember a Thanksgiving memory or big feasting holiday, one of which you had alot to eat…

> *The meal practically lasted all day. There was laughter and feasting, and at the end, a very full stomach. If someone tried to offer you some more dessert or a taste of some more mashed potatoes, you sighed and said with pain, "No way, not one more bite!"*

Well, think of this spiritually, physically and emotionally—spirit, soul and body! In Jesus Christ, God has made us to be complete. He didn't want one thing missing. Now, that is the perfect gift!

> *"For in him dwelleth all the fulness of the Godhead bodily.*[9] *And ye are complete in him, which is the head of all principality and power."*[10]

Colossians 2:9-10

"For in Him the whole fullness of Deity (the Godhead) continues to dwell in bodily form [giving complete expression of the divine nature].[9] And you are in Him, made full and having come to fullness of life [in Christ you too are filled with the Godhead—Father, Son and Holy Spirit—and reach full spiritual stature]. And He is the Head of all rule and authority [of every angelic principality and power]."[10]

Colossians 2:9-10 Amplified

The Greek word for "Complete" is "Pleroo," which comes from the root word "Pleres," meaning, "to make replete, to cram and to level up; to fill up, cause to abound" (Strong's #4137 from #4134).

Replete: *1. Abundantly supplied, provided 2. Stuffed, gorged with food and drink 3. Complete (Webster's Dictionary).*

"Pleroo" is shown in the New Testament nearly one hundred times as "fulfill, fill, full."

When you think of Jesus or when you picture Him, it's not just Jesus. It's also Elohim, which means Gods; it speaks of the plural form, referring to the Trinity. We know there is only one God, but three persons in one: the Father, Son and Holy Spirit. All the fullness of the Godhead dwells inside Him. So, my friend, I know it's hard to fathom, but all the fullness of the Godhead lives inside you, too. You can meditate on this one thought for an eternity, and feed off of it. Once you get ahold of this, watch out, world! There will be no stopping what you can do for God! He will use you greatly! It was His own choice to come and live in side you forever—to never, ever leave.

The World Cannot Make You Complete

Some people think they will be complete when they get that big house they've been waiting on. Others think that it's a mate who will finally bring them happiness and completion. Some are looking at their outward appearance, seeking plastic surgery and youthfulness to make them complete. Whether it's fame, power or money… these will not bring completion or happiness. Ask any of those people who have reached these heights. There's only One who can make you fully complete. He is the *only* Way, the Truth and the Life. That is Jesus Christ.

He Has Showered You

"Grace and peace be multiplied unto you through the knowledge of God, and of Jesus our Lord,² According as his divine power hath given unto us all things that pertain unto life and godliness, through the knowledge of him that hath called us to glory and virtue."³

2 Peter 1:2-3

He hasn't just cleansed your sins or paid for your eternal life. You have been given everything, including His Kingdom and His Sonship. But if you don't get into His word and find out what you have already been given, you will never enjoy being an heir. The best and most wonderful "news" is that we can have fellowship now with our Father, the Almighty Jehovah God.

"Blessed be the God and Father of our Lord Jesus Christ, who hath blessed us with all spiritual blessings in heavenly places in Christ.³ According as he hath chosen us in him before the foundation of the world, that we should be holy and without blame before him

in love:[4] *Having predestinated us unto the adoption of children by Jesus Christ to himself, according to the good pleasure of his will,*[5] *To the praise of the glory of his grace, wherein he hath made us accepted in the beloved.*[6] *In whom we have redemption through his blood, the forgiveness of sins, according to the riches of his grace;*[7] *Wherein he hath abounded toward us in all wisdom and prudence;*[8] *Having made known unto us the mystery of his will, according to his good pleasure which he hath purposed in himself."*[9]

Ephesians 1:3-9

You have to meditate on the Word in order to plant these living, powerful seeds into your heart and mind. It's the only way to get revelation—understanding, not just head knowledge. If you realize that knowing Jesus and the Father is the only way to true joy, and that "in Jesus" you are complete, then you should be gobbling up the Word to find out what you already have in the Spirit. For it is now that we can experience life "in Christ." It is now that we can be satisfied.

We don't have to wait for anything else to be happy. The best thing for us has already happened. Satisfaction is at its height when you come to the realization that Christ lives in you, and that you can have a relationship with Him. Nothing, no one, no goal or quest can compare to this grand achievement of what God has done.

God the Father sees you "in Christ." He doesn't look at your shortcomings and imperfections. He sees righteousness, completion and holiness. He sees Jesus. He loves you and your uniqueness, and He sees you through Jesus. This is very humbling. It is not based upon our performance, but on the performance of Jesus on the cross. We are the receivers of His wonderful grace.

You should never again say that God doesn't love you because now you can see that isn't true. The Father planned that Christ would be in you long before the foundations of the world were ever made. Jesus obeyed this plan to the end. He obeyed because of His love for the Father and His love for us. The Holy Spirit rose Jesus from the dead, and is now quickening your mortal body by His Spirit that lives in you (Romans 8:11)…because you are His.

Chapter 12

WHAT PLEASES YOUR FATHER?

Faith is like radar that sees through the fog.

-Corrie Ten Boom

Once you discover what pleases God your Father, you will want to do all that you can to please Him, and you'll find it's not hard at all. It pleases Him when you believe His Word and trust in Him simply; like a child.

God Delights in You Knowing Him

The word *"Delight"* in the Webster's dictionary is very interesting: *A high degree of gratification. Joy. Extreme satisfaction. Something that gives pleasure.*

I want to share a favorite Old Testament passage of mine. As you think about this verse, you will see that God's view is so different from this world's view of who and what is really important. This passage explains something God delights in:

> *"Thus saith the Lord, Let not the wise man glory in his wisdom, neither let the mighty man glory in his might, let not the rich man glory in his riches:[23] But let him that glorieth glory in this, that he understandeth and **knoweth** me, that I am the Lord which **exercise** lovingkindness, judgment, and righteousness, in the earth: for in these things I delight, saith the Lord."[24]*
>
> ***Jeremiah 9:23-24***

"Knoweth." We have seen this word earlier, which is "Yada" (Strong's #3045), speaking of the *intimate knowing*. You realize that God knows about you in great detail. But He wants you to *know* Him. He wants you to know that He is FULL of lovingkindness. When you understand this truth, it gives Him such great delight.

The word ***"Exercise"*** is the Hebrew word "Asah" (Strong's #6213), which is used 1333 times in the Old Testament meaning "Do," and 653 times, "Make." In this

Scripture, "Exercise" is interpreted as such: "To make, in the broadest sense and widest application. To accomplish, bear, advance, appoint, bestow, bring forth, be busy, have the charge of, execute, fashion, finish, be industrious, perform and practice." To exercise implies a continual action; a practice. So God the Father is continually exercising lovingkindness.

Now let's focus on the the word *"Lovingkindness"* or "Khehsed," which is translated as "Mercy" 149 times. The Hebrew word "Khehsed" is speaking of kindness, rarely reproof, beauty and favor. "To do a good deed or to be loving and merciful, to have pity" (Strong's #2617).

Someone can be kind and open a door for you just to be polite, or even return something that you've lost to be kind. But what this is speaking of goes far beyond kindness. It is with affection. It is kindness with agape love. Think back on the times you have given in love, not expecting anything in return. You did it just because you loved someone. "Agape" love is the God kind of love. It's a self-sacrificial love. When you bless others with the motivation of love, it gives God great pleasure.

Now let's look at the last word, ***"Delight,"*** in this passage: it comes from the Hebrew word "Kapevf," and is used 39 times; also used as "Please" 14 times and "Desire" 9 times. "Kapevf" means, "to incline to, to bend, to be pleased, desire, favor, like, be moved, be well pleased, to take pleasure" (Strong's #2654).

The point of reading Jeremiah 9:24 is not to inspire us to say, "Oh great, we get to get things!" God desires to meet your needs, but that is not the ultimate. Think of an earthly parent; as a child, what is the ultimate thing you could get from your parents? Quality time—that feeling of total unconditional love and acceptance. Nothing monetary or material could ever take the place of this. Ask anyone who is incarcerated in prison. Deep in our hearts, what we all want is the same; to be loved and accepted. We want to know that our life matters. So next time you read this verse, remind yourself that the God of this universe also wants to have your time and your love; a close relationship with you. Your life matters to Him. His greatest desire is an intimate friendship that no money can buy. All of His acts of lovingkindness bring you closer to Him. It would give Him pleasure if our hearts' desire was to know Him.

"What I want most is to be with you, Lord, to know you more. All the other stuff is just icing on the cake. But you, God, knowing you, is the cake."

For some, it's more like this:

"If you would have mercy on me, if you could find it in your heart to help me..."

How in the world would you feel if your kids did that to you? How ridiculous would that sound to you? How ridiculous it must sound to God; it must grieve Him!

To Walk in Christ Pleases God

He gave His best to us, which was a huge sacrifice—Jesus Christ, the Son of God! And Jesus fully obeyed. Through His finished work on the cross, we can now come into fellowship with the Father with confidence. Be thankful and grateful that as He exercises His lovingkindness towards us, it gives Him great pleasure. Feel free to brag about it! Not, "Look what God did for me, and not for you." Brag about His goodness, His righteousness, His mercy, His forgiveness, and His tender love to all!

It is very humbling to receive something we didn't deserve. The sacrifice of Jesus paid it all! The wrath of God was placed on Him instead of us. Jesus took all of our sins and sicknesses in His body to set us free. When we believe and receive these truths, and begin to walk in them, it pleases our Father tremendously. It is the richest gift He has ever given. If you dare to believe it, you will walk in the blessing of it all.

Here are more verses concerning *His delight*, detailing what God takes pleasure in. You may be surprised at how they unveil His ways and love for truth and life.

"A false balance is abomination to the Lord: but a just weight is his delight."

Proverbs 11:1

"Lying lips are abomination to the Lord: but they that deal truly are his delight."

Proverbs 12:22

"The sacrifice of the wicked is an abomination to the Lord: but the prayer of the upright is his delight."

Proverbs 15:8

"Righteous lips are the delight of kings; and they love him that speaketh right."

Proverbs 16:13

"Let them shout for joy, and be glad, that favour my righteous cause; yea let them say continually, Let the Lord be magnified, which hath pleasure in the prosperity of his servant."

Psalm 35:27

"The Lord taketh pleasure in them that fear him, in those that hope in his mercy."

Psalm 147:11

"For the Lord taketh pleasure in his people: he will beautify the meek with salvation."

Psalm 149:4

"Yet it pleased the Lord to bruise him; he hath put him to grief: when thou shalt make his soul an offering for sin, he shall see his seed, he shall prolong his days, and the pleasure of the Lord shall prosper in his hand.[10] *He shall see of the travail of his soul, and shall be satisfied: by his knowledge shall my righteous servant justify many; for he shall bear their iniquities."*[11]

Isaiah 53:10-11

"Fear not, little flock; for it is your Father's good pleasure to give you the kingdom."

(Which He did through Jesus.)

Luke 12:32

"Having made known unto us the mystery of his will, according to his good pleasure which he hath purposed in himself."

Ephesians 1:9

"For it is God which worketh in you both to will and to do of his good pleasure."

Philipians 2:13

"Wherefore also we pray always for you, that our God would count you worthy of this calling, and fulfil all the good pleasure of his goodness, and the work of faith with power."

2 Thessalonians 1:11

"Thou art worthy, O Lord, to receive glory and honour and power: for thou hast created all things, and for thy pleasure they are and were created."

Revelation 4:11

God takes NO pleasure in these:

"Have I any pleasure at all that the wicked should die? saith the Lord God: and not that he should return from his ways, and live?[23] For I have no pleasure in the death of

him that dieth, saith the Lord God: wherefore turn yourselves, and live ye."[32]

Ezekiel 18:23,32

"Now the just shall live by faith: but if any man draw back, my soul shall have no pleasure in him."

Hebrews 10:38

"But without faith it is impossible to please him: for he that cometh to God must believe that he is, and that he is a rewarder of them that diligently seek him."

Hebrews 11:6

Why is it impossible to please Him without faith? This is the way God lives, so get used to it. He is a God of faith, so His children also must be. We get everything He gave to us through faith. He has gone through much sacrifice to bring us back to Him. For us to decide not to partake of this new life by faith is to say, "We don't really believe in Him…we don't trust Him."

Faith is a gift to us. We can choose to use it. Once you know what pleases Him, you will want to point yourself in that direction.

And you'll be pleased, too! Joy will abound, knowing that you are pleasing your Father. You have the ability to please the God of the universe!

Know Your Covenant

He is a Covenant God who keeps all of His promises; He will not break any of them. Nor will He ever break His covenant with us. It pleases Him that you understand and walk in His Covenant.

> *"My covenant will I not break, nor alter the thing that is gone out of my lips.[34] Once have I sworn by my holiness that I will not lie unto David.[35] His seed shall endure for ever, and his throne as the sun before me.[36] It shall be established for ever as the moon, and as a faithful witness in heaven. Selah."[37]*
>
> **Psalm 89:34-37**

The "seed" He is talking about is Jesus.

> *"Now to Abraham and his seed were the promises made. He saith not, And to seeds, as of many; but as of one, And to thy seed, which is Christ."*
>
> **Galatians 3:16**
>
> *"And if ye be Christ's, then are ye Abraham's seed, and heirs according to the promise."*
>
> **Galatians 3:29**

The Scriptures above are speaking of covenants with David and Abraham, but we are partakers of these as well through faith in Jesus Christ. No man has ever been able to keep the Ten Commandments. No man was perfect enough. No man could follow the law perfectly, except for one man—Jesus. Only He could keep the law perfectly. He was God in the flesh. God loved us so much, that He came down in the flesh to Earth to make a better covenant that could never be broken; because the One who made it was God.

> *"But now hath he obtained a more excellent ministry, by how much also he is the mediator of a better covenant, which was established upon better promises.*[6]

What Pleases Your Father?

For if that first covenant had been faultless, then should no place have been sought for the second."⁷

Hebrews 8:6-7

In the Old Testament God made covenants with Abraham, Moses and David. We can enjoy them now through faith in Christ Jesus, but the New Covenant is that which we should be living in. It is the New Covenant that Jesus established by giving up His life on the cross. In the Old Testament, animal sacrifices were offered up every year for the sins of the people, so that they could be forgiven. But it was only temporary, as the payments for sin had to be offered up continuously.

The reason the New Covenant is better, is because this time Jesus was the sacrifice. He was the only One needed for all the sins of all the people around the world—past, present and future. He was the ultimate, perfect lamb that was slain. This covenant was not initiated by a mere human to God. For whenever God would make a covenant with man, man proved himself incapable to keep his end of the bargain because his flesh was weak. This New Covenant was made by God, Who came to Earth and was born in the flesh.

This New Covenant was made by God through Jesus for us. This means it is perfect and unbreakable. It is a sure covenant that will last forever.

Understanding the New Covenant and your covenant rights as a believer in Jesus will make a big difference in your life by knowing what you are entitled to as a believer. All the promises of God will be cemented into your heart and mind when you know you have a sure agreement with God through Jesus Christ.

Think of the love of God. He knew we were imperfect, so He provided the perfect sacrifice for us. Someone had to die for our sins, so He chose to spare us by giving His Son in our place. Jesus paid for everything. He paid for our sicknesses, our sins, our poverty, our shame, our torment and damnation to hell; our sorrow, our loneliness, and the list goes on and on. Through Jesus, we now have peace and forgiveness with God. It pleases your Father when you make a choice to discover these truths for yourself. This New Covenant is now based on love and grace. If we walk in God's love, we fulfill all the commandments. Love must be our motivation, as it is God's.

Walking in love is walking in the light, so you will not stumble, because the light is on! His love will keep you safe from the enemy (1 John 2:10), but you are the one who has to choose to walk in love.

"For the law was given by Moses, but grace and truth came by Jesus Christ."

John 1:17

"For this is the covenant that I will make with the house of Israel after those days, saith the Lord; I will put my laws into their mind, and write them in their hearts: and I will be to them a God, and they shall be to me a people:[10] *And they shall not teach every man his neighbour, and every man his brother, saying, Know the Lord: for all shall know me, from the least to the greatest.* [11] *For I will be merciful to their unrighteousness, and their sins and their iniquities will I remember no more."*[12]

Hebrews 8:10-12

When you receive the New Covenant by faith, it will please God immensely. I encourage you to find some good teaching on your covenant relationship with God. Learn about the different covenants in the Old Testament, and focus on the New Covenant in the New Testament. The benefits of fully receiving everything provided by the New Covenant with God are invaluable, and they will change your life.

Chapter 13

LIVING IN THE FAITH REALM OF THE FATHER

Faith is taking the first step. You don't have to see the whole staircase.

-Martin Luther King, Jr.

"Now unto him that is able to do exceeding abundantly above all that we ask or think, according to the power that worketh in us."

Ephesians 3:20

*E*verything you receive from God is first received by faith in the Spirit. God is a Spirit, and they that worship Him must worship Him in Spirit and in truth. He is a limitless God that is eternal, even as His love for you is eternal, but you must learn to see and grasp Him with your spiritual eyes. We have such an exciting future filled with wonderful adventure. He has taken care of everything, but you must act in faith, as God does. His ways are all about faith.

> *"And I heard a great voice out of heaven saying, Behold, the tabernacle of God is with men, and he will dwell with them, and they shall be his people, and God himself shall be with them, and be their God.[3] And God shall wipe away all tears from their eyes; and there shall be no more death, neither sorrow, nor crying, neither shall there be any more pain: for the former things are passed away.[4] He that overcometh shall inherit all things; and I will be his God, and he shall be my son."[7]*
>
> *Revelation 21:3-4,7*

> *"And he shewed me a pure river of water of life, clear as crystal, proceeding out of the throne of God and of the Lamb.[1] In the midst of the street of it, and on either side of the river, was there the tree of life, which bare twelve manner of fruits, and yielded her fruit every month: and the leaves of the tree were for the healing of the nations.[2] And there shall be no more curse: but the throne of God and of the Lamb shall be in it; and his servants shall serve*

him:³ And they shall see his face; and his name shall be in their foreheads.⁴ And there shall be no night there; and they need no candle, neither light of the sun; for the Lord God giveth them light: and they shall reign for ever and ever."⁵

Revelation 22:1-5

When it speaks of overcoming in verse 7, it's talking about the one who trusts and believes in God's Word. The one who refuses to throw away His faith and confidence in the Word of God—He has chosen to live by faith.

Live in the Spirit

It is vital that you understand who you really are. Yes, we live on this earth in a physical body. God has blessed us with five senses to experience life: to learn and enjoy; taste and see; touch, hear and smell. We see in the physical realm, which is where we are. Everything we know and have memories of, we have experienced through our physical senses.

We are also spiritual beings. You have a physical body, but you also have a spiritual body. Just because you don't see it, doesn't mean it's not there. It's what causes you to move and live on this earth. Think about it. When you go to a funeral and see the deceased person in the casket, their body is still there, right? But their life is gone somewhere else. Their spirit has left the body, and without it, they cannot have life here on this earth.

We are eternal beings; every single person on this earth will live eternally. It just differs where they will be, depending upon whom they choose to serve and believe in, God or Satan. If you don't choose Jesus, the only other option is Hell. There are no other choices.

So, if we have our physical body that we experience and enjoy in this present life, we need to remember that we also have our spiritual body. Just like our physical body has arms, a face, eyes, ears, and legs, our spiritual bodies do, as well. Since God is Spirit, and we are to relate and worship and receive Him in the Spirit, doesn't it make sense then, that we should get to know that realm?

Let's go a step further. Those of us who are hungry for God and His Word, to know our Savior and to serve Him, you would think that living in the spiritual realm and seeing with our eyes of faith would be far more real than the physical realm, wouldn't you? Stay with me, now. I am not proposing that we get weird, but the spiritual world is more real than the physical. In fact, it is through the Spirit that the physical was created. This physical world is a by-product of the Spirit. Remember in Genesis Chapter 1, that this world was created by God imagining it and seeing it in the Spirit, and then speaking it into existence?

> *"Through faith we understand that the worlds were framed by the word of God, so that things which are seen were not made of things which do appear."*
>
> **Hebrews 11:3**

> *"If we live in the Spirit, let us also walk in the Spirit."*
>
> **Galatians 5:25**

> *"If ye then be risen with Christ, seek those things which are above, where Christ sitteth on the right hand of God.[1] Set your affection on things above, not on things on the earth."[2]*
>
> *Colossians 3:1-2*

Live By Faith

It is required of us, as children of God, to live by faith. The just shall live by faith (Hebrews 10:38). You do have a choice. If you want to live God's way, God's life, in God's realm, then you must forget about being led by your feelings. Feelings go up and down—they cannot be trusted. We are expected to live higher than that. We are expected to live by God's Word, for it is truer than our feelings could ever be. His Word is even truer than all of your circumstances.

Remember the picture of the seagulls flying down below, poking through the garbage? You were not meant to be a seagull. You were meant to live by faith, seeing through your eyes of faith like your Father, as an eagle soaring high above the clouds of life. Seeing things that are not, as though they were. Envisioning your future. Seeing with your heart according to what God's Word says about you. That is how you really are. We should get into the habit of seeing so clearly with our hearts (our eyes of faith), that the unseen world is more real to us than the physical world in which we live. Again, this is where we can use our imaginations, and allow them to work for us in a positive way.

Abraham Walked By Faith

Let's look at an example of one of our great fathers, Abraham. He learned to see with eyes of faith. His focus was narrow-minded in a positive way, only on God's promises.

> *"Who against hope believed in hope, that he might become the father of many nations, according to that which was spoken, So shall thy seed be.[18] And being not weak in faith, he considered not his own body now dead, when he was about an hundred years old, neither yet the deadness of Sarah's womb:[19] He staggered not at the promise of God through unbelief; but was strong in faith, giving glory*

> *to God;[20] And being fully persuaded that, what he had promised, he was able also to perform.[21] And therefore it was imputed to him for righteousness."[22]*
>
> *Romans 4:18-22*

You see, God told Abraham that he would be the father of many nations, and that he would have a son to start that line. But Sarah was unable to have any children because she was barren. Besides that, they were both old and past their child-bearing years. Every morning, Abraham was reminded of his age; he could see his old, wrinkly hands. He had to trust God. He didn't deny his circumstances, but he chose to "consider them not." That means he chose to take his eyes off of them. All he chose to focus on is God's promise, and that He was able to perform what He had said. He chose to see with eyes of faith.

> *"And he brought him forth abroad, and said, Look now toward heaven, and tell the stars, if thou be able to number them: and he said unto him, So shall thy seed be.[5]*

And he believed in the Lord; and he counted it to him for righteousness."[6]

Genesis 15:5-6

You see, God gave Abraham hope. When he would look at the stars, that vision would help him to dream, to use his imagination and see through the eyes of His heart. That vision became so clear and vivid in Abraham's eyes that he became strong in faith, giving glory to God. It was so clear, as he only focused on the goal, that He became fully persuaded that what God had promised, He was able also to perform. You can't look at the circumstances and believe God's Word at the same time. It just won't work!

Flood Your Mind With His Word

We are capable of seeing with our eyes of faith because of what we have in Christ. Are you fully persuaded as to what you are believing God for? This should be our goal; it should be where we live. We are different—we may live on this earth, but through Jesus, we are not of this world. Our interests should be His interests. What moves His heart should move ours. His thoughts should be our thoughts. This is the realm of the Father.

To get there, you must fill your heart and mind with His Word. You must press through and meditate on His Word. You will know when you reach this place, and here are just a few things that will happen. You will wake up in the middle of the night with a Scripture flowing through your mind, and as you drift back to sleep, it will minister to you. The Holy Spirit will reveal the Word to you. You might wake up in the morning with a worship song playing in your head, and there is no radio on. The Holy Spirit will unveil the Word to you as you become comfortable meditating on His Word. Different Scriptures will come together like pieces of a puzzle; and you will see them put together as if they were paintings—pictures of revelations that only He could give to you.

God speaks to us through His Word. So, if you want to hear Him speak, learn His Word, and keep it before you. He is not going to speak through thoughts of worry, strife, lust or begging. You don't have to be tormented by the devil. He has already been defeated. Set your mind on things above.

"My son, attend to my words; incline thine ear unto my sayings.[20] Let them not depart from thine eyes; keep them in the midst of thine heart.[21] For they are life unto those that find them, and health to all their flesh.[22] Keep thy heart with all diligence; for out of it are the issues of life."[23]

Proverbs 4:20-23

The more you meditate on His Word, the more peace you will have. Health will come to your body, and restoration to your soul. The Word of God has the power to change you. Trust in it, and renew your mind by it. You will grow in the love and compassion of God as you pursue your relationship with Him. You will see how naturally compassion flows. You won't be able to help it; love reaches out, just as God did to you, and brings forth compassion. God's Love overflows.

I remember leading worship at a rescue mission, when the compassion of God came over me for this young couple. The young girl was pregnant and they were homeless. They had finished their meal and sat down, waiting for the service to start. I didn't even think about whether they would be offended or not, but an overwhelming urge came over me to lay hands on her belly, and to pray for her baby. So I did, and without thinking twice I said, "Can I pray for your baby?" Like an instant reflex, they both held hands and also laid their hands on her tummy. They were so grateful.

The love of God will cause you to be bold. There is boldness in His love. This is God's realm. There will be times when you and I may feel alone; times when we are hungry for His presence, and eager to meet with Him. There may be times when we don't physically feel Him there, but desire to hear His sweet voice. Remember this: God is not in your physical realm, nor in your feelings. You won't find Him there, so stop thinking He has left you. It is spirit to spirit, remember that. You must use your faith, and reach out to Him in the Spiritual realm. God is there, and His Spirit is in you.

> *"That they should seek the Lord, if haply they might feel after him, and find him, though he be not far from every one of us."*

Acts 17:27

He Longs to Fellowship With You

He's the one Who said He will never leave you nor forsake you. You are the one who has to make a decision out of your own free will to believe Him. That He is looking at you, listening to you and loving you. You can have as much of God's attention as you want. He's always there ready to listen, but don't start begging. I truly believe that is the wrong way to go about things. Begging is not activating your faith. In fact, it is the opposite, showing that you are not in faith. A child hops up on his parent's lap and puts his arms up, expecting to be held. Just know that He is there, already listening. All you have to do is talk to Him. Here is an example:

> *"Lord, I know that you are here listening—thank you for that. Thank you for loving me. You have given me all things in Christ. Father, I want to spend this time with You. I want to fellowship with You. So right now, even though I may not feel You, I know that You're here, and I will talk as if You are. I want to tell You that I appreciate how You've*

> *been taking such good care of me. I receive Your wisdom in my life. Thank You for Your love."*

Now, forget about everything else, and take some time to listen. Hear Him speak. Fellowship is a two-way street. It's not just about you doing all the talking. But when you do talk, your attitude must be an attitude of faith and praise, because everything is already done. There is no need to whine or beg; to demand or be angry. If you are doing these things, then you still don't understand that He is Love. God is Love, and He will reach out to you in love.

Even if He corrects you through His Word, it's still in love. If a person truly knew that His Heavenly Father was there waiting for Him, thinking of Him with enduring love, watching and listening, how do you think this person would respond? I believe He would readily and eagerly come to God with no hesitation. For the Father simply and dearly LOVES YOU.

Chapter 14

RECEIVE JESUS AS YOUR SAVIOR

You have a free choice to receive Jesus Christ as your Lord and Savior. This is the most important decision you'll ever make!

> *"That if thou shalt confess with thy mouth the Lord Jesus, and shalt believe in thine heart that God hath raised him from the dead, thou shalt be saved.[9] For with the heart man believeth unto righteousness; and with the mouth confession is made unto salvation."[10] How then shall they call on him in whom they have not believed? and how shall they believe in him of whom they have not heard? and how shall they hear without a preacher?"[14]*
>
> ***Romans 10:9-10,14***

> *"For by grace are ye saved through faith; and that not of yourselves: it is the gift of God."*
>
> ***Ephesians 2:8***

Like a child, just believe and receive. Jesus already did all the work. It's so much easier to come to God when you understand that He is a good God Who loves you no matter what. He accepts you right now as you are. You don't have to clean up first—Jesus will do that for you.

If you would like to receive Jesus Christ into your heart, all you have to do is pray this simple prayer:

"Lord Jesus, I confess that You are my Lord and Savior. I believe in my heart that God raised You from the dead. By faith in Your Word, I receive salvation now. I give you my life. Thank you for saving me!"

If you meant that with your heart, you are now saved, Dear One. Remember, it has nothing to do with your feelings, only the decision you've made. Now that you are born again, you are brand new!

"Therefore if any man be in Christ, he is a new creature: old things are passed away; behold, all things are become new."

2 Corinthians 5:17

Receive the Holy Spirit

When Jesus rose again to be at the right hand of the Father, He didn't want us to be alone. He told the disciples to wait—that the Father would send a Comforter to be with them; a helper. As you read the Scriptures and see for yourself that He is from God, you can take comfort in that this is a blessing. He only wants the best for us, and we need not be afraid of anything given by God, because He loves us. The Holy Spirit is a gift from God.

"But when the Comforter is come, whom I will send unto you from the Father, even the Spirit of truth."

John 15:26

"Howbeit when he, the Spirit of truth, is come, he will guide you into all truth: for he shall not speak of himself;

but whatsoever he shall hear, that shall he speak: and he will shew you things to come."

John 16:13

"But ye shall receive power, after that the Holy Ghost is come upon you: and ye shall be witnesses unto me both in Jerusalem, and in all Judaea, and in Samaria, and unto the uttermost part of the earth."

Acts 1:8

The Word explains how they were filled:

"And they were all filled with the Holy Ghost, and began to speak with other tongues, as the Spirit gave them utterance."

Acts 2:4

And you must know that the Holy Spirit is still for us today because:

"Jesus Christ [is] the same yesterday, and to day, and for ever."

Hebrews 13:8

"For every one that asketh receiveth; and he that seeketh findeth; and to him that knocketh it shall be opened.[10] *If ye then,...know how to give good gifts unto your children: how much more shall your heavenly Father give the Holy Spirit to them that ask him?"*[13]

Luke 11:10,13

If you would like to receive the precious Holy Spirit, all you have to do is ask, believe and receive. Just pray this simple prayer:

"Father, I recognize my need for Your power to live this new born-again life. Fill me with Your Holy Spirit. By faith, I receive Him right now! Thank You for baptizing me. Holy Spirit, You are welcome in my life in the name of Jesus."

It's that simple. The Holy Spirit is a gentleman, and He won't come uninvited. You are filled with God's supernatural power. Some syllables from a language you don't recognize will rise up from your heart to your mouth. You may not hear anything, so by faith then, speak a continuous sound out loud. The Holy Spirit will help you, just ask Him. As you speak the sounds out by faith, you will be releasing God's power from within you by building yourself up in the Spirit. No man understands these words, but God. You are speaking God's mysteries, Spirit to Spirit.

You may only have one word at first—just give it some time and practice. Just like a little child learns to speak a language, they start with a word or two at a time. Make a habit of praying in tongues. You may think, "I'm only praying one word." But in God's eyes and according to His word, you are speaking the wisdom of God for your life and for others. It will bless you.

> *"For he that speaketh in an unknown tongue speaketh not unto men, but unto God: for no man understandeth him; howbeit in the spirit he speaketh mysteries."*
>
> **1 Corinthians 14:2**

"He that speaketh in an unknown tongue edifieth himself."

1 Corinthians 14:4

"For if I pray in an unknown tongue, my spirit prayeth, but my understanding is unfruitful."

1 Corinthians 14:14

You can do this whenever and wherever you like. You can pray for your loved ones, and for the many situations in which you need wisdom. It really doesn't matter whether or not you felt anything when you prayed to receive the Lord and His Spirit. If you believed in your heart that what God's Word says is true, then God's Word says you did receive. What a wonderful new journey you have embarked on. Seek the Lord, and He will show Himself real to you.

Don't wait to enjoy God's promises until you finally reach heaven. Live today as He planned for you to live. Enjoy His promises; enjoy His presence, His love, His sweet fellowship and conversation. You will see that there is nothing that can compare to it—nothing. No one, nothing, no amount of money, fame or material goods can satisfy the craving in your heart; that perpetual longing only Jesus can fulfill, that only the love of the Father can meet. Take it, child, it's yours.

> *"I am the root and the offspring of David, and the bright and morning star.*[16b] *And the Spirit and the bride say, Come. And let him that heareth say, Come. And let him that is athirst come. And whosoever will, let him take the water of life freely."*[17]
>
> *Rev 22:16b-17*

My hope from writing this book is that you will come to know the Father, whether it's for the first time, or if it is your desire to nurture and develop a stronger love-walk with Him. I pray that you will seek Him with all your heart and find Him: the One Who loves you so deeply and unconditionally, Who is longing for you to get to know Him. I pray that this book will help change the view that some people have had about Him, that people will know and understand that He is a God of goodness, mercy and grace.

After reading this book, I hope you see that God is Love, and that He tenderly loves you, treasures you and wants you to know Him intimately. He wants us to spend now and eternity getting to know Him. It is going to take an eternity to learn how wonderful His mercy is. Praise God! He has already pursued you—now, it's your turn to respond.

Respond to the Father's Love...

About the Author

Linda Patarello is a born again Christian, and graduate from Charis Bible College in Colorado Springs, Colorado. She currently lives there, and spends most of her time spreading the truth about God's Love from the written Word. Linda is a California native with broad experience in leading praise & worship and songwriting. She believes that the highest calling is to worship the "Giver of All Gifts." She also believes we are born to pursue a relationship with God the Father, Jesus Christ and the Holy Spirit, and to share it with others. Her vision is to help people find true love for the Word of God, and to uncover its precious truths that are waiting to be revealed.

For More Information or to Contact the Author, Please Write to:

Linda Patarello
P.O. Box 7964
Colorado Springs, CO 80933
www.Heartsower.com

Prayer of Salvation

There is nothing more fulfilling in life than knowing that God loves you. God has made, and continues to make His love known to us by having sent His only begotten son, Jesus Christ, to die on the cross as payment for our sins and the injustices done unto us.

Has anyone willingly given up their life in exchange for yours, so that you may live? Jesus did. "Greater love hath no man than this, that a man lay down his life for his friends" (Jn. 15:13). Notice, that Jesus said this *before* he went to the cross. He laid down His life for us because he saw you and I, his friends, benefiting from this act of love.

You were the joy that was set before Jesus. "For the joy that was set before him [he] endured the cross, despising the shame, and is set down at the right hand of the throne of God" (Heb. 12:2). Only a true, selfless friend could love like this. Would you like to know the One Who finds you valuable, Who truly loves you? If you would like to ask Jesus to be your friend and your Lord and Savior, you can ask Him today. You can use your own words or pray,

"Lord Jesus, I want to know you, I want to be your friend. I invite you into my life, so that I may know you more. Be my saving friend, Lord and Savior. I am sorry for all my sins and past mistakes. Thank you for forgiving me and loving me, in spite of my past. You are my friend, even when I have no one else. I want to receive everything you have for me, even your Holy Spirit. Take control of my life, and through my relationship with you, let it grow and mature, and become a light unto others. Thank you for freeing me from sin and darkness, and for putting me in right-standing with you forever. I am saved! Thank you, Jesus! Amen!

If you prayed this prayer for the first time in your life, we believe that you were born again! Find a good Bible-based church, and connect with other believers. Please share your testimony or visit us online:

http://www.orionproductions.tv/contact-us.html

You can write to us:

Orion Productions

PO Box 51194
Colorado Springs, CO 80949

Blessings to you! From our staff at Orion Productions.

To make known the stories and accounts of God's work in people's lives through multimedia products and services.

Our latest publishing information can be found by visiting our website at:

www.orionproductions.tv/publishing.html

www.ingramcontent.com/pod-product-compliance
Lightning Source LLC
Chambersburg PA
CBHW071701090426
42738CB00009B/1614